The Math of Astrology

A Step-by-step Guide

Peter Murphy, M.A., LL.B., PMAFA
Beth Rosato, MAFA, D.F. Astrol.S

Formerly Titled: *The Math of Chart Construction*

ISBN-10: 0-86690-456-5
ISBN-13: 978-0-86690-456-8

Third Edition: 2011

Cover Design: Jack Cipolla

Published by:
American Federation of Astrologers, Inc.
6535 S. Rural Road
Tempe, AZ 85283

www.astrologers.com

Printed in the United States of America

Contents

Preface

The intent of this book is to offer a simple, methodical guide to the construction of a natal chart without recourse to a computer program. Much that has been written on the subject is complicated by unnecessary technical detail, often to the point of incomprehensibility. It is little wonder that many people are deterred from studying chart construction, feeling that a doctorate in mathematics or astronomy must surely be a prerequisite for such a complex endeavor. The truth is that chart construction, while admittedly calling for concentration and a methodical approach, is not all that difficult, and need not be made to appear so. It is open to anyone with basic arithmetical skills, and a little time and patience.

Many may wonder, in this age of rampant technology, why anyone would take the time to learn an ancient, but apparently abstruse skill. There are a variety of answers to this question. The simplest are that some people still have to work without a computer, and that manual chart construction is required for the examinations set by the accrediting bodies in the field of astrology. An even better reason is that chart construction is satisfying and fun to do. But there is also a more profound reason. Astrology is not just a matter of hurriedly churning out information. To analyze a chart thoroughly and with understanding involves getting inside the chart with every facet of your being. And, although this can be accomplished during the process of analysis, there is no doubt that, on some level, the process of constructing a chart, of working it through its various stages, of seeing it gradually spring to life from the data and worksheets, gives you a feel for the chart, the sense of personal involvement with the sacred information it represents.

We have assumed that our readers have a basic understanding of the planets, signs, and houses, the cycles and retrograde motions of the planets, the nature of the zodiacal wheel, the nodes of the Moon, the Part of Fortune and the Part of Spirit. Except for this essential astrological knowledge, we have kept technical information to a minimum. We hope you find chart construction rewarding and enjoyable.

From Peter: I would like to thank my co-author, Beth, for her enthusiasm and support for this project, my astrology teacher, Kimberly McSherry, for everything she taught me, and my wife, astrology partner, and friend, Chris, for her unfailing love and support in everything I do, including much help with this book.

From Beth: I would like to thank my co-author, Peter, for the pleasure it has been working on this project together. I would also like to thank Jesse and Angelica, who always believe in me. Sharing life's journey with you is a privilege and a joy. I would like to acknowledge *Dell Horoscope* Editor-in-Chief Ronnie Grishman, Editor Edward Kajowski, and Associate Editor Jack Pettey for permission to use some material previously published in *Horoscope*, Vol.60, No.4 (April 1994), "The ABCs of Chart Analysis" by Beth Koch. And, on a personal note to our readers, I would like to whisper an encouraging, "C'mon, you can do it!"

Peter Murphy
Bellville, Texas

Beth Rosato
Long Island, New York

Preface to Revised Edition

Almost as soon as this book was first published, both the authors and publishers were rather mystified about why we had limited it to the math of natal chart construction. An understanding of the math involved in progressions and transits is a valuable source of insight for any astrologer, and is essential for success at the higher levels of professional examinations. Here then, is a more complete treatment of the subject. The material on progressions includes the necessary preliminary calculations, the construction of a complete progressed chart, and the timing of progressed events such as sign changes, contacts to natal planets and points, and lunations. We have also offered an overview of the interpretation of progressed charts. A final chapter deals with a miscellany of matters involving calculation, transits, solar and lunar returns, aspects, midpoints and declinations.

As before, we hope that a mastery of these techniques will bring not only the satisfaction of accomplishment, but also a greater sense of connection with the charts and lives of astrologers and their clients.

Peter Murphy
Bellville, Texas

Beth Rosato
Long Island, New York

Authors' Note

The ephemeris references in this book are taken from *The American Ephemeris for the 20th Century*. As regards planetary positions and ingresses, this ephemeris is based on Universal Time (UT), which is essentially equivalent to Greenwich Mean Time (GMT). Students may later work with *The American Ephemeris for the 21st Century* or the *Rosicrucian Ephemeris* in which planetary positions and ingresses are based on Terrestrial Dynamical Time (TDT). TDT is based on certain geophysical factors which affect the length of a terrestrial day, and which cannot be calculated precisely in advance, but it tends to run a little over fifty seconds ahead of UT. This difference, known as Delta Time or DT, must be added to UT to produce TDT. When calculating planetary positions and ingresses using TDT values, for most accurate results DT should be added to the Greenwich birth time before interpolation. Except in the case of the Moon, however, any discrepancy resulting from failure to do this is insignificant for normal purposes. There is no difference between ephemerides in the expression of sidereal time, which is always calculated in UT, so that no adjustment need be made when calculating house cusps.

Chapter 1

Getting Ready

To learn the mechanics of chart construction, we will work with the birth data of a fictitious person called Jane Doe. She was born at Austin, Texas on May 20, 1945 at 11:42 p.m. We will construct a natal chart for her without using a computer calculation program. After this, we have provided four practice exercises for you to work on. We have also included the completed worksheets and charts for these exercises, so that you can check your calculations in detail.

Tools

PENCIL, RULER, AND PAPER. You will need plenty of paper. After you have worked through the book, it will probably occur to you that having a series of pre-made worksheets would be a good idea. These are not difficult to make, once you know what you are doing. You can see those designed by Peter Murphy in the answers to the practice exercises; you may wish to modify them or design your own. However, ordinary paper will do. Use a pencil. You are going to make a lot of mistakes, and an eraser is vital so that you can make corrections easily and quickly. In addition to drawing lines, the ruler can help your eyes focus on the data in the various books we will be using. The print used in the various tables is rather small, and the thickness of the ephemeris can cause the pages to bend in such a way that the lines can otherwise be hard to follow consistently.

CALCULATOR. Any calculator that can perform the basic four arithmetical functions will do. Memory function is useful, but not essential. Of course, if you regard this as a violation of the no-computer rule (which it is not) or if you just like to do arithmetic by hand, by all means do it the hard way. But be warned. We are going to be doing a lot of decimalization of numbers in a 60 base. So, personally, we will be using our calculators.

ATLAS. This is not an atlas with maps, but a book which lists cities, arranged by state, and gives their geographical coordinates (latitude and longitude) as well as certain other important information. ACS Publications publishes both: *The American Atlas*, which you will use for all births in the United States, and *The International Atlas*, which you will use for all births elsewhere in the world.

MIDNIGHT GREENWICH EPHEMERIS. An ephemeris is a book which records the positions of the planets, and other astronomical data, from day to day. ACS Publications publishes a complete ephemeris for the 20th century. You may also wish to invest in one for the 21st century, now available up to the year 2050.

The data in the midnight Greenwich ephemeris are based on the planetary positions at midnight Greenwich Mean Time (GMT) at Greenwich, England, on each day. This, of course, is not the only possible point of reference. Indeed, many astrologers work with an ephemeris based on noon instead of midnight. But experience has shown that this causes unnecessary complications. Once you learn with a midnight ephemeris, you will quickly adapt to the noon version if you have to. Greenwich is taken as a base because, by tradition, degrees of longitude

1

are measured from Greenwich, and other time zones around the world are defined as being so many hours behind (earlier than) or ahead of (later than) GMT. This is true, not only for astrology, but for all purposes of travel, navigation, communications and so on.

TABLES OF HOUSES. A book of tables is a book which, among other things, gives tables of the cusps of the houses, based on the latitude of the place of birth and the sidereal (star) time of birth. The sidereal time of birth is calculated based on data given in the ephemeris, as we shall see later. The tables give the house cusps for the tenth through the third houses. The cusps of the fourth through ninth houses will, of course, be exactly opposite, so they need not be calculated separately. For example, if the cusp of the Ascendant is 14 Gemini 36, then the cusp of the Descendant will be 14 Sagittarius 36, and so on around the wheel.

There are several versions of the house system, the most commonly used being Placidus, a medieval system, and Koch, a more modern system. Both have their devotees, but they are equally valid, and ACS Publications publishes editions of both. In this book, we shall use Placidus, but the method of calculation using the Koch tables would be exactly the same.

Some astrologers use what is called the equal house system. This involves taking a starting point, usually the Ascendant, and making the houses equal in size around the wheel. For example, if the Ascendant is 14 Gemini 36, then the cusp of the second house would be 14 Cancer 36, the cusp of the third 14 Leo 36, and so on. Although this prevents consideration of the relative sizes of the houses and eliminates intercepted signs, you still need the tables of houses to calculate your starting point.

The Zodiac. All these systems are based on what is called the tropical zodiac, which is the zodiac used almost universally in western astrology. A "zodiac" is simply a two-dimensional representation of the apparent movement of the planets about the ecliptic through the twelve zodiacal signs, by means of which their positions can be tracked at any given time. The basis of the tropical zodiac is seasonal. It assumes that the first day of spring (the Vernal Equinox) corresponds each year to a solar position of zero degrees of Aries, and assigns positions to the planets in the signs accordingly. There are many possible variants. The most important alternative is the sidereal zodiac, used in Indian astrology and by a small minority of western astrologers. The sidereal zodiac takes into account the astronomical fact of the precession of the equinoxes, and assumes (correctly, from an astronomical perspective) that the Vernal Equinox does not remain constant at zero degrees Aries or any other fixed point. In fact, it precesses "backwards" through the signs at a rate of about one degree every seventy-two years. This means that, today, the Vernal Equinox occurs at about seven degrees Pisces. There is strong historical evidence to suggest that the zodiac has been adjusted from time to time through the ages to take account of this. However, adherents of the tropical zodiac point out that astrology is a symbolic system and argue that linkage to the seasons is an important part of our whole philosophy of astrology. The debate about the "correct" zodiac is complex, but as astrologers on both sides of it seem to obtain excellent results using their preferred zodiac, we will simply follow the general western practice and use the tropical zodiac.

One final point: The tables of houses used in the United States are based on latitudes in the Northern Hemisphere. If you are dealing with a birth in the Southern Hemisphere, you can still use them, but you must remember to make certain corrections, which we will mention as we work through our example.

BLANK WHEELS. You will need these to produce the final chart from your calculated data. They are readily obtainable commercially or you can design your own to incorporate other information such as aspects, elements, and qualities in whatever way you find most helpful.

Data Required to Calculate A Chart

To calculate a natal chart, you must know the date, clock time, and place of the subject's birth. Additionally, you must then find the geographical coordinates (latitude and longitude) of the place of birth and ascertain whether local Standard Time (ST) was operating there at the time of birth. So first, let's see how we can obtain this information.

DATE, CLOCK TIME AND PLACE OF BIRTH. This information is generally obtained from the subject. It has been a source of frustration for as long as natal astrology has been practiced. For example, William Lilly, a seventeenth-century English astrologer, wrote the following in the mid-1640s, yet many a modern astrologer reads his words with an understanding nod of the head:

"Many men and women have not the time of their nativities, or know how to procure them, either their parents being dead, or no remembrance being left thereof; and yet for divers weighty considerations they are desirous to know by a question of astrology."—[*Christian Astrology*, pub. 1647]

Usually, the date and place are not a problem, although there are some people who have inadequate information even about these. Clock time is more often an issue. By clock time, we mean simply the time which a clock at the place of birth would have recorded as the birth time. Later, we shall have to convert clock time in various ways, but we have to start with it. Do not ask the client for anything more specific. It is your job as the astrologer to figure out whether it was ST or not, and to calculate the equivalent time GMT.

For births in the United States, birth certificates are probably the most reliable source of information. Many foreign certificates do not contain time information. All birth certificates are fallible; they all depend on the input of a fallible human being in recording the time—a human being, moreover, for whom time was not exactly the first priority in the circumstances. There are occasionally other problems, too. For example, if you look at the atlas section for Illinois, it will tell you that state law required births to be recorded in Central Standard Time until July 1, 1959, but that this law was not always observed! Nonetheless, you should accept the information on a birth certificate as being the best available. Experience has shown that it is usually acceptably accurate.

If the subject cannot get a birth certificate, or if the certificate does not contain the information (or is from Illinois), you have to look for anecdotal evidence such as the recollections of relatives. The mother is not the ideal person for this—she had other things on her mind at the time—but fathers often remember and other relatives can often recall receiving a telephone call "in the middle of dinner," or when "the Mets were up 3-2 in the middle of the eighth," and so on. The fact of the matter is that we have to work with whatever we can get. Fortunately, a birth is a very memorable event in most families and, one way or another, we can usually get acceptable information. In those cases where we cannot, adjustment or rectification may be the only solution.

In our case, we are fortunate in having accurate information. Jane Doe was born at Austin, Texas, on May 20, 1945 at a clock time of 11:42 p.m. Note this information on your worksheet.

LATITUDE AND LONGITUDE OF BIRTH PLACE. We need these data for accurate calculation of the house cusps, including the Ascendant and Midheaven, and for accurate birth time calculation. Latitude is a measurement by degrees, minutes, and seconds of how far north or south (N or S) of the equator any given place is. Longitude is a measurement by degrees, minutes, and seconds of how far the place is east (E) or west (W) of the Greenwich Meridian (from which longitude is traditionally measured).

This information is obtained directly from the atlas, which gives the latitude and longitude of Austin, Texas. An occasional problem arises when the subject was born in some village or hamlet too small for inclusion in the atlas. This tends to happen more frequently in *The International Atlas*, used for non-U.S. births. In this case, ask the subject for the name of the nearest town of any size, and use that, bearing in mind that it is an approximation. Or look at a map of the area which includes the place of birth and make your own approximation. A second occasional problem arises when there are two towns of the same name in a state. This also tends to occur only with smaller communities. The atlas provides a solution to this problem by telling you the county in which each town is situated. For example, just to the right of the word Austin is the number 227. This refers to a list at the beginning of the section for Texas in which the counties are identified by number. So, provided the client knows either the county of birth, or the name of the nearest large town, you should be able to identify the birth place precisely.

In our case, we have no such difficulty. The atlas shows that Austin is at latitude 30N16′01″ (i.e. 30 degrees, 16 minutes, 01 second N of the Equator) and longitude 97W44′34″ (i.e. 97 degrees, 44 minutes, 34 seconds west of the Greenwich Meridian). Write this information on your worksheet.

TIME IN OPERATION AT THE DATE, TIME, AND PLACE OF BIRTH. The world is divided into time zones, each of which has a "standard time" measured relative to GMT as so many hours, or fractions of hours, either east (later than) or west of (earlier than) GMT. When it is necessary to distinguish, the practice is to write times later than GMT with a minus sign (-) and times earlier than GMT with a plus sign (+). For example, a time shown as -7:00:00 would be seven hours later than GMT.

3

It is essential to know in which time zone your birth occurred. Time zones change at certain longitudes east or west of Greenwich, which are known as meridians; a new Standard Time begins at each meridian. The meridians are separated by fifteen degrees of longitude, which is the equivalent of one hour of time (although certain parts of the world also use time differences of half an hour). The meridians affecting births in the United States (all west of Greenwich) are shown in Figure 1.

A more complete table of time zones for the rest of the world will be found at the end of the chapter. The practical consequence of the time zones, as everyone knows who has ever reached out and touched someone through transatlantic communication, is that when it is 11:00 p.m. in London (GMT), it is only 6:00 p.m. in New York City (EST), 5:00 p.m. in Austin (CST), 4:00 p.m. in Denver (MST), and 3:00 p.m. in Los Angeles (PST).

The meridians do not, of course, correspond with state or national boundaries. For obvious reasons of convenience, states and nations frequently opt to use a uniform time zone, despite being divided by one or more meridians. For example, California is bisected by the PST Meridian (120W00) but the entire state uses PST. Although Los Angeles is at longitude 118W14′34″ (east of the PST Meridian) and San Francisco is at longitude

Figure 1

Time zone	Meridian	Hours W of GMT
Eastern Standard Time (EST)	Longitude 75W00	5 hours W of GMT
Central Standard Time (CST)	Longitude 90W00	6 hours W of GMT
Mountain Standard Time (MST)	Longitude 105W00	7 hours W of GMT
Pacific Standard Time (PST)	Longitude 120W00	8 hours W of GMT

122W25′06″ (west of the PST Meridian), both use PST. This is not always the case, however, because the size of the state or nation may render it impracticable to maintain the same ST throughout. There are four time zones operating in the United States, and while most of the State of Texas uses CST, some parts of it, including the city of El Paso, use MST. So it is important always to check the atlas. You cannot assume that a time zone applies merely because the birth occurs in a particular state or nation.

BIRTHS DURING DAYLIGHT SAVINGS OR WAR TIME. The picture is complicated when the birth occurred during Daylight Time (DT) or War Time (WT). If you recall the old mnemonic "Spring Forward, Fall Back," it will become obvious that, for any place west of Greenwich, DT or WT reduces the time difference from GMT by one hour and, for any place east of Greenwich, increases the difference by one hour. Now, please note carefully: Whether or not DT or WT was in operation at *Greenwich* is irrelevant. Our ephemeris is based on Greenwich Mean Time, so this will be a constant. Only variations in the time operating at the *place of birth* matter. So, while DT (or WT) is in operation in the United States, remember that EDT (or EWT) is only four hours west of GMT, CDT (CWT) only five hours, MDT (MWT) only six hours, and PDT (PWT) only seven hours. We will see later how to deal with this in our calculations.

FINDING OUT WHAT TIME WAS OPERATING. As noted above, it is essential to refer to the atlas, and not to make assumptions based on the state or nation of birth. The method is as follows. Go back to the page of *The American Atlas* for Austin. Immediately before the latitude for Austin, you will see the number 1. The number 1 refers to the state time tables, which are found at the beginning of each state section in *The American Atlas*. If you turn to the beginning of the Texas section in the atlas you will see that there are three possible time tables to consult for Texas. The number 1 for Austin directs us to the first of these. (Some states have considerably more than three, but always look at the one given for the city in question.) Now, look in Texas Table 1 for Jane Doe's birthday. You will see that it falls between two dates, in an entry which looks like this.

2/09/1942	02:00	CWT
9/30/1945	02:00	CST

What this tells us is that on February 9, 1942 at 2:00 a.m., this part of Texas began using Central War Time and that this continued until September 30, 1945 at 2:00 a.m., when it reverted to Central Standard Time. As Jane was born on May 20, 1945, it follows that CWT was in operation in Austin, Texas, at the time of her birth. Note this on your worksheet.

Before we leave this, look at the top and bottom of the table. At the top, you will see that in earlier times, before the modern system of meridians was developed, Local Mean Time (LMT) was used. These times were generally the equivalent of the modern meridian standard times, but there were many variations, and the possibility of some degree of error must be accepted in dealing with these older births. At the bottom, you will see that on April 30, 1967 at 2:00 a.m., this part of Texas adopted one of the standard United States time tables. Different parts of the country did this at different times, as times across the country gradually became standardized. The Texas table indicates that U.S. Table 1 was adopted. This means that, for a birth at Austin after 2:00 a.m. on April 30, 1967, you would refer to U.S. Table 1. The U.S. tables (of which there are five) are found on the inside covers of the atlas.

TIME ZONE CORRECTION. This is an important piece of information to be used in birth time calculation. It can be obtained directly from the atlas. If you look again at the page of the atlas for Austin you will see the figures 6:30:58 after the latitude and longitude for Austin on the right side of the page. This is the time zone correction (TZC), a measurement of time—6 hours, 30 minutes, 58 seconds. This is exactly how far behind GMT the time at Austin, Texas is when the local ST (CST) is operating there. So, the TZC tells us two things:

- The time difference between Greenwich and Austin in hours, minutes and seconds (the total correction).
- The time difference between Austin and the CST meridian in minutes and seconds (the local correction).

Why do we need to know this? We already know that CST is six hours west of GMT; hence, the six hours in the TZC total correction for Austin. But this is not quite precise enough. Although Austin is within the Central Standard Time Zone, it is not situated exactly on the Central Standard Time Meridian. This is obvious, because the CST Meridian is at longitude 90W00, whereas Austin is at longitude 97W44′34″. So, Austin is 7 degrees, 44 minutes, 34 seconds west of the CST Meridian. This means that, at any given moment, the true local time at Austin will be somewhat earlier than it would be at a point exactly on the Meridian. The TZC local correction tells us how much earlier—in this case 30 minutes, 58 seconds. Note the TZC on your worksheet.

Although the TZC can be taken from the atlas, it can also be calculated by means of the simple formula of multiplying the longitude of the place of birth by four minutes. This will give you the TZC in minutes, which you can then convert to hours, minutes and seconds. Before trying this, you might want to read the hints for calculation below. Why do we multiply by four minutes? Because if one meridian (or 15 degrees of longitude) = 1 hour, then each degree of longitude = 4 minutes of time. For example, EST (75W00) is exactly 15 degrees, or 1 hour (4 x 15 = 60 minutes) from CST (90W00) which is why EST is one hour later than CST.

Useful Hints for Calculation

CALCULATIONS IN 60 BASE. It will already be obvious that we are going to be doing a lot of calculations in a 60 numerical base. Both time (hours, minutes, and seconds) and longitude (degrees, minutes, and seconds) are expressed in base 60: 60 seconds = 1 minute; 60 minutes = 1 hour or degree. In one way, this is very helpful, because it means that we can combine measurements of time and measurements of longitude in our calculations, as in the case of the TZC. At the same time, however, we do have to deal repeatedly with base 60. So, before beginning, it is worth considering the easiest way to do so, given that our calculators (and our minds) operate most naturally in a 10 (decimal) base.

It is not too difficult. Let's take an example. By the way, five decimal places, which is within the range of all calculators, is adequate for all normal chart construction purposes. Let's suppose we want to multiply 6 hours (or degrees) 30 minutes, 58 seconds by 2.45. The easiest way is to decimalize the time/degrees before calculation, and to reconvert the decimalized answer to minutes/seconds after calculation. To decimalize a number in 60 base, divide the number by 60. To reconvert a decimalized answer, multiply by 60. These processes, of course, are performed only with the minutes and seconds (the numbers after the decimal point)—the hours or degrees are whole numbers which are the same either way.

So, our procedure is:

1. Divide the seconds by 60.

2. Express the minutes and seconds as a decimal and divide it by 60.

3. Express the hours, minutes and seconds as a decimal—this is the number to be multiplied.

4. Multiply by 2.45.

5. Reconvert the decimalized answer to minutes and seconds by multiplying by 60.

(1) 58 seconds/60 = 0.96666 of a minute

(2) Therefore: we have 30.96666 minutes

30.96666/60 = 0.51611 of an hour

(3) Therefore: we have 6.51611 hours

(4) 6.51611 x 2.45 = 15.96446 hours

(5) To complete, we reconvert 0.96446 into minutes and seconds.

0.96446 x 60 = 57.8676 minutes
0.8676 x 60 = 52.056 seconds

Rounding off, the answer is 15 hours, 57 minutes, 52 seconds.

If this is not comfortable at first, practice a little before moving on. We shall be doing a lot of calculations of this kind as we go along. For convenience, Figure 2 shows a table of whole numbers between 1 and 59, divided by 60 to 5 decimal places.

USE OF THE 24-HOUR CLOCK. If you can adapt to using the 24-hour clock in your calculations, you will eliminate many possibilities of error. This is because we calculate times from a given base (in our case, midnight, because we are using a midnight ephemeris) and it is vital not to confuse a.m. and p.m. times. Obviously, such confusion is likely to result in an error of twelve hours in our calculations. The 24-hour clock will never confuse you. If you do not have a military or navigation background, in which case you will be familiar with this system already, all you need to do is use the table in Figure 3. The 24-hour clock is based simply on one period of 24 hours, rather than two periods of 12 hours.

In the 24-hour clock system, times are written in three columns—hours, minutes and seconds. Jane Doe's birth time, expressed in the a.m./p.m. clock would be written in the familiar form of 11:42 p.m. Using the 24-hour clock, it would be written as 23:42:00. Because the 24-hour clock eliminates the risk of some very serious errors, we shall use it in this book from this point on.

Figure 2—Whole Numbers Divided by 60					
1. 0.01666	11. 0.18333	21. 0.35	31. 0.51666	41. 0.68333	51. 0.85
2. 0.03333	12. 0.2	22. 0.36666	32. 0.53333	42. 0.7	52. 0.86666
3. 0.05	13. 0.21666	23. 0.38333	33. 0.55	43. 0.71666	53. 0.88333
4. 0.06666	14. 0.23333	24. 0.4	34. 0.56666	44. 0.73333	54. 0.9
5. 0.08333	15. 0.25	25. 0.41666	35. 0.58333	45. 0.75	55. 0.91666
6. 0.1	16. 0.26666	26. 0.43333	36. 0.6	46. 0.76666	56. 0.93333
7. 0.11666	17. 0.28333	27. 0.45	37. 0.61666	47. 0.78333	57. 0.95
8. 0.13333	18. 0.3	28. 0.46666	38. 0.63333	48. 0.8	58. 0.96666
9. 0.15	19. 0.31666	29. 0.48333	39. 0.65	49. 0.81666	59. 0.98333
10. 0.16666	20. 0.33333	30. 0.5	40. 0.66666	50. 0.83333	

Figure 3—Operation of 24-Hour Clock System			
24-hour clock	a.m./p.m. clock	24-hour clock	a.m./p.m. clock
00:00:00	12:00:00 a.m. (midnight)	12:00:00	12:00:00 p.m.(noon)
01:00:00	1:00:00 a.m.	13:00:00	1:00:00 p.m.
02:00:00	2:00:00 a.m.	14:00:00	2:00:00 p.m.
03:00:00	3:00:00 a.m.	15:00:00	3:00:00 p.m.
04:00:00	4:00:00 a.m.	16:00:00	4:00:00 p.m.
05:00:00	5:00:00 a.m.	17:00:00	5:00:00 p.m.
06:00:00	6:00:00 a.m.	18:00:00	6:00:00 p.m.
07:00:00	7:00:00 a.m.	19:00:00	7:00:00 p.m.
08:00:00	8:00:00 a.m.	20:00:00	8:00:00 p.m.
09:00:00	9:00:00 a.m.	21:00:00	9:00:00 p.m.
10:00:00	10:00:00 a.m.	22:00:00	10.00:00 p.m.
11:00:00	11:00:00 a.m.	23:00:00	11:00:00 p.m.

We are now ready to work through the stages of chart construction. The stages are as follows.

Stage 1: Preliminary birth time calculations

Stage 2: Preliminary sidereal time calculations

Stage 3: Calculating the house cusps

Stage 4: Calculating the planetary positions

Stage 5: Calculating the Part of Fortune and the Part of Spirit

Stage 6: Detecting and correcting errors

Stage 7: Copying the data on to the blank wheel

Always follow this order of procedure.

Figure 4—World's Principal Time Zones West of Greenwich		
Standard Time	**Meridian**	**Time from GMT (hrs/mins)**
Greenwich	00:00	00:00
Azores	15W00	01:00
	30W00	02:00
East Brazil	45W00	03:00
Newfoundland	52W30	03:30
Atlantic	60W00	04:00
Eastern	75W00	05:00
Central	90W00	06:00
Mountain	105W00	07:00
Pacific	120W00	08:00
Yukon, Alaska	135W00	09:00
Hawaii	150W00	10:00
Samoa	165W00	11:00
International Date Line	180W00	12:00

Figure 5—World's Principal Time Zones East of Greenwich		
Standard Time	**Meridian**	**Time from GMT (hrs/mins)**
Greenwich	00:00	00:00
Central European	15E00	01:00
Egypt, Finland	30E00	02:00
Baghdad, Russia Zone 1	45E00	03:00
Russia Zone 2	60E00	04:00
Pakistan, Russia Zone 3	75E00	05:00
India	82E30	05:30
Bangladesh, Russia Zone 4	90E00	06:00
Burma	97E30	06:30
Java, Indochina	105E30	07:00
China, W. Australia	120E00	08:00
Japan	135E00	09:00
S. Australia	142E30	09:30
E. Australia, Guam	150E00	10:00
Solomons	165E00	11:00
New Zealand	180E00	12:00

Chapter 1, Questions and Answers

What is Latitude?

Answer: A measurement by degrees, minutes and seconds of how far north or south a place is of the equator.

What is Longitude?

Answer: A measurement by degrees, minutes and seconds of how far east or west a place is of the Greenwich Meridian.

What is Greenwich Mean Time?

Answer: The Standard Time at the Greenwich Meridian, England, from which longitude is measured.

What is Local Standard Time?

Answer: The time at a given place based on its distance in longitude from Greenwich, and expressed as so many hours (or fractions of hours) behind or ahead of Greenwich Mean Time, the formula being one hour of time = 15 degrees of longitude.

What is a Meridian?

Answer: A meridian is an imaginary line running north to south, linking all places at which a new standard time zone begins. Meridians are separated by 15 degrees of longitude, and are measured from the meridian at Greenwich.

What is Daylight or War Time?

Answer: Variations of standard time adopted in some places for the purpose of maximizing daylight at certain times of year, or during war time. This has the effect of reducing the difference between local time and Greenwich Mean Time by one hour for places west of Greenwich, and increasing the difference by one hour for places east of Greenwich.

What is Time Zone Correction?

Answer: The difference between the time at a given place and Greenwich Mean Time, expressed in hours, minutes and seconds. The minutes and seconds also relate to the difference in time between the place and a point exactly on the local standard meridian.

How do I find the Latitude and Longitude of a place?

Answer: These are given in the atlas opposite the name of the city.

How do I find whether Standard Time was operating on the date of birth?

Answer: Look for the number immediately to the left of the latitude. Find the state time table corresponding to that number, and find the subject's date of birth in the table. The letters ST, DT or WT will tell you what time was operating. The letters E, C, M or P will tell you the time zone. If the U.S. Tables apply, these are given in the inside covers of the atlas.

What is the formula for calculating Standard Time if the birth time was Daylight or War Time?

Answer: Deduct one hour.

What is the formula for decimalizing minutes and seconds?

Answer: Decimalize the seconds by dividing by 60. Express the minutes and seconds as a decimal, and divide that by 60.

What is the formula for converting a decimalized number of hours (or degrees) back into minutes and seconds?

Answer: Multiply the number after the decimal point by 60. The whole number will be the minutes. Multiply the number after the decimal point by 60 to give the seconds. Round off to the nearest second.

What is the formula for calculating the Time Zone Correction?

Answer: Decimalize the longitude of the place of birth, and multiply by four. This gives the answer in minutes. Convert to hours, minutes and seconds.

Chapter 2

Preliminary Birth Time Calculations

In constructing a chart, it is always advisable to have in front of you all the data produced so far. In our case, our worksheet will look like this. All the details are important. Leave nothing out.

Name: Jane Doe

Date of Birth: May 20, 1945

Time of Birth: 23:42:00 CWT

Place of Birth: Austin, Texas

Latitude: 30N16'01"

Longitude: 97W44'34"

Time Zone Correction: 6:30:58

The first stage is to do two simple preliminary calculations using the clock birth time. These calculations will provide us with two important pieces of information for later use. The first of these is the birth time expressed as GMT, based on Standard Time at the local meridian (CST). The second is the True Local Time (TLT) at the place of birth (Austin) as opposed to the time at the CST Meridian.

GMT BIRTH TIME. We need to know the GMT birth time, because we are using a Greenwich ephemeris to calculate our planetary positions. We already know that Jane was born in the Central Standard Time Zone, and that CST is six hours behind GMT. So, if the birth time were 23:42:00 CST, we would conclude that the GMT birth time would be six hours later, that is to say at 05:42:00 GMT. But, in this case, CWT was operating. So, we must deduct one hour from the clock time to arrive at the time expressed in ST. Remember that the GMT birth time must always be based on local *standard* time.

Thus: 23:42:00 CWT
         - 1:00:00
         22:42:00 CST

Now, all we have to do is add six hours, which gives a GMT time of 04:42:00.

DATE OF BIRTH AT GREENWICH. But please notice one more thing of critical importance, which is true of many afternoon and evening births in the United States. The GMT time relates to the day *after* Jane's American birthday. She was born at 22:42:00 CST on May 20, but the GMT equivalent is 04:42:00 on *May 21*.

In fact, any birth occurring at or after 18:00:00 CST (or 19:00:00 EST, etc.) will have a GMT equivalent in the early morning of the following day. Always look to see whether the GMT calculation changes the date. For evening American births, which are always west of Greenwich, the effect will always be to go ahead into the next day. With early morning births east of Greenwich, the reverse would be true. In any event, it is essential to note this, because when we come to use the Greenwich ephemeris for our planetary calculations, our starting point will be May 21, not May 20. So, the notation on our worksheet should read:

GMT birth time: 04:42:00 GMT, May 21, 1945.

TRUE LOCAL TIME AT BIRTH PLACE. Jane was born at a clock time of 23:42:00 (CWT). But this is not quite precise enough for our purposes. The same time of 23:42:00 would have been indicated by a clock if Jane's birth had occurred at any place operating on CWT, i.e. any place between longitudes 90W00 and 105W00. Yet, because time varies with longitude, it is clear that the precise time could not have been 23:42:00 throughout the Central Time Zone, which encompasses fifteen degrees of longitude. In fact, 23:42:00 was the precise time only at places on the Central Meridian itself. The precise time at any place west of the Central Meridian must have been somewhat earlier than 23:42:00, and the precise time at any place east of the Meridian somewhat later.

Jane was born, not on the Central Meridian, but at Austin, which is at longitude 97W44'34 or, in other words, 7 degrees, 44 minutes, 34 seconds west of the Central Meridian. We have already seen that the local correction of the TZC tells us how much earlier it is in Austin than at a point exactly on the Central Meridian. This time difference is 30 minutes, 58 seconds earlier. Therefore, by deducting 30 minutes, 58 seconds from the CST birth time, we can calculate the precise time of Jane's birth at Austin. This is known as the True Local Time (TLT) of birth. But once again, just as in the GMT calculation, remember that we must work with Standard Time, so don't forget to deduct the 1 hour for WT, to arrive at 22:42:00.

Birth in clock time:	23:42:00 CWT
- 1 hour for WT	1:00:00
Birth in ST	22:42:00 CST
- Time zone correction	00:30:58
TLT at Austin =	22:11:02 CST, May 20, 1945

Make a note of this on your worksheet.

This calculation, however, is not always so straightforward. It so happens that Austin is west both of Greenwich *and* of the CST meridian. So, by deducting the local correction of the TZC, we will always arrive at the correct TLT. But it is possible that a birth place may be west of Greenwich, but *east* of the local ST meridian. For example, Los Angeles operates on PST, but is at longitude 118W14'34, E of the PST Meridian at 120W00. A diagram (Figure 6) may help to show the difference.

The atlas gives the TZC for Los Angeles as 7:52:58, which is correct as a statement of how far Los Angeles is west of Greenwich. But, because, unlike Austin, Los Angeles is east of its local meridian, the 52:58 is not the appropriate local correction. Because the PST Meridian is eight hours west of Greenwich, but Los Angeles is only 7:52:58 west of Greenwich, the local correction will be (8:00:00 - 7:52:58) = 0:07:02. And, because TLT in Los Angeles will be somewhat later than the time at the PST Meridian, the proper procedure is to add 7:02 to the PST birth time. It is vital always to think what you are doing, not just do it mechanically. You are working out whether the time at the place of birth is later or earlier than the time at the local ST meridian, and this must depend on whether the place of birth is east or west of the meridian.

It is not difficult to recognize such cases. In the case of Austin, the total TZC correction has the same number of hours (six) as the CST Meridian, whereas the total correction for Los Angeles (seven) has one hour less than the PST Meridian (eight), indicating that the Meridian must be further west of Greenwich than Los Angeles.

The same thing happens in reverse where you have a birth place which is east of Greenwich but also west of the local ST meridian. In this case, the time at the place of birth will be somewhat earlier than at a point exactly on the

Figure 6			
(W) Austin (97W44'34")	CST Meridian (90W00)	Greenwich (0)	(E)
PST Meridian (120W00)	Los Angeles (118W14'34")	Greenwich (0)	

meridian, so you would deduct a correction of the difference in minutes and seconds between the birth place and the meridian.

There is a simple method of cross-checking your GMT and TLT calculations, which we recommend you always use. If you add TLT to TZC (for births west of Greenwich) or subtract TZC from TLT (for births east of Greenwich) you will arrive at the birth time expressed in GMT. Thus, in Jane's case:

TLT	22:11:02
+ TZC	06:30:58
= GMT	28:42:00 or 04:42:00 the following day GMT.

If this cross-check does not produce the right result, one or both calculations must be in error.

Chapter 2, Questions and Answers

What is the true local time of birth?

Answer: The precise time at the birth place, as opposed to the clock time operating at that place, which is actually the time at the local standard meridian. The true local time will be somewhat earlier than the time at the meridian for places west of the meridian, and somewhat later for places east of the meridian.

What is the formula for calculating the birth time expressed as GMT?

Answer: Express the birth time in local standard time (if necessary, deduct one hour for DT or WT for births west of Greenwich, or add one hour for births east of Greenwich). Add (west of Greenwich) or subtract (east of Greenwich) the number of hours between local standard time and GMT. If in doubt as to the number of hours, use one hour for each fifteen degrees of longitude between the local standard meridian and Greenwich (or consult the table of world time zones). As a cross-check, for births west of Greenwich, add TLT and TZC, or, for births east of Greenwich, subtract TZC from TLT. This should produce the same GMT time. Check to see if birth date has changed for GMT birth time.

Calculating TLT?

Answer:

1. Obtain the TZC from the Atlas, or calculate by multiplying the longitude by four to get the TZC in minutes, then converting to hours, minutes and seconds.

2. Adjust for DT or WT, to produce ST birth time.

3. (a) Place west both of Greenwich and local meridian: deduct minutes and seconds of TZC from ST birth time.

   (b) Place east both of Greenwich and local meridian: add minutes and seconds of TZC to ST birth time.

   (c) Place west of Greenwich, but east of local meridian: deduct total TZC from number of hours local standard time is earlier than GMT, and add difference to ST birth time.

   (d) Place east of Greenwich, but west of local meridian: deduct total TZC from number of hours local standard time is later than Greenwich, and deduct difference from ST birth time.

Chapter 3

Preliminary Sidereal Time Calculations

W e now have to calculate what is called the "sidereal" or "star" time of birth. It is unnecessary to go into much technical detail about what sidereal time is. Suffice it to say that sidereal time is not related to the time of birth as calculated on earth. Rather, it is a measurement of time based on the rotation of the earth with respect to the stars. It is essential to calculate it accurately if we are to arrive at the correct house cusps. Indeed, sidereal time is a foundation for the house cusps.

Sidereal time is expressed as a continuous 24-hour clock, so it runs from 0:00:00 to 23:59:59, at which point it starts over again. The midnight ephemeris gives the sidereal time at midnight on any given day, and the tables of houses tells how the house cusps change with intervals of sidereal time of four minutes. But, because not all births conveniently occur at midnight, or at an exact multiple of four minutes from 0:00:00, we obviously have to make adjustments to find the exact sidereal time and then adjust the cusps accordingly. We begin by calculating the exact sidereal time for Jane Doe's birth. This is done by taking the sidereal time at Greenwich for the midnight before TLT, and then adjusting it to correspond to (1) the longitude of the place of birth, and (2) TLT.

Step 1

Find sidereal time at Greenwich at the midnight preceding TLT. This information is found in the ephemeris in the first column for the appropriate birth date. (The page for May 1945.) The rule is to take the sidereal time for the midnight preceding TLT, even if the GMT birth date falls on the following day. Therefore, we do not have to worry about the difference between TLT and GMT because we are going to make an adjustment for the difference in longitude between Greenwich and Austin in just a moment. Jane's TLT is 22:11:02 on May 20, 1945. The preceding midnight is midnight on May 20, 1945. The ephemeris gives the sidereal time for this date as 15:49:08. Note this on your worksheet.

Step 2

Correct midnight sidereal time for longitude of place of birth. Next, we make what is called a longitude correction to compensate for the fact that Austin is at a longitude west of Greenwich. The formula for calculating the longitude correction is quite simple. Add 10 seconds for every 15 degrees Austin is west of Greenwich. The most convenient way to do this is simply to add two-thirds (10/15) of the longitude of Austin to the midnight sidereal time. The longitude for Austin is 97W44'34", so we calculate two thirds of 97:44:34. Decimalized, 97:44:34 converts to 97.74277. Two-thirds of this is 65.16184 seconds, which is about one minute, five seconds. (The longitude correction can never be more than two minutes.) We now add the longitude correction to the midnight

13

sidereal time, to produce a corrected sidereal time.

Midnight sid. time   15:49:08
+ longitude correction   1:05
Corrected sid. time   15:50:13

If you are working with a birthplace east of Greenwich, subtract the longitude correction from the midnight sidereal time, instead of adding it.

Step 3

Adjust corrected sidereal time to correspond with TLT rather than GMT. The next step is to adjust the corrected sidereal time from midnight GMT to correspond with the TLT of birth. To do this, you add to the corrected sidereal time (1) the interval between the TLT and the previous midnight, and (2) a correction of that interval of ten seconds per hour (one second per six minutes).

Jane's TLT is 22:11:02, so the interval from the previous midnight is also 22:11:02. This is where you will be really glad you are using the 24-hour clock. If you are using a.m./p.m., please remember that, for a p.m. birth you must add 12 hours; the interval between 10 p.m. and the preceding midnight is 22 hours, not 10 hours!

To this interval, we also add a correction of 10 seconds per hour, which is called "acceleration." Twenty-two hours gives us 220 seconds. Additionally, we have a little over 11 minutes. Ten seconds per hour works out to one second per six minutes, so the correction for our 11 minutes comes out to about two seconds. That is as precise as we need to be. So our total correction is 222 seconds, or 3 minutes, 42 seconds.

Sidereal time never goes beyond 23:59:59. At this point, it starts over, so if the answer comes out to more than 24 hours (which it clearly will in our case), deduct 24 hours from the total.

Corrected sid. time   15:50:13
+ interval TLT-previous midnight: 22:11:02
+ acceleration   3:42
Exact sid. time =   38:04:57
- 24 hours   24:00:00
Calculated sid. time =   14:04:57

Note this on your worksheet.

BIRTHS IN THE SOUTHERN HEMISPHERE. Finally, note that if you are dealing with a birth in the Southern Hemisphere, you can use exactly the same method but you must add a further 12 hours to the calculated sidereal time. In our example, this would produce an exact sidereal time of 26:04:57, from which we would deduct 24 to arrive at the calculated sidereal time of 02:04:57.

Chapter 3, Questions and Answers

What is Sidereal Time?

Answer: Sidereal time is a measurement of time based on the rotation of the earth with respect to the stars. Therefore, it also measures the changes in house cusps. It is expressed as a 24-hour clock, which runs continuously from 0:00:00 to 23:59:59. It is unrelated to events on earth.

What is the formula for calculating Sidereal Time?

Answer:

1. From ephemeris, take sidereal time for midnight previous to TLT.

2. Calculate longitude correction of two-thirds longitude of place of birth (10 seconds for every 15 degrees). Add for births west of Greenwich, subtract for births east of Greenwich.

3. To this, add:

    (a) interval between TLT and previous midnight; and

    (b) acceleration of this interval at rate of 10 secs/hour, and 1 sec/6 mins.

4. If total hours exceeds 24, deduct 24.

5. For births in Southern Hemisphere, add 12 hours, and, if total hours exceeds 24, deduct 24.

Chapter 4

Calculating the House Cusps

As we have noted already, the tables of houses provides us with the house cusps at intervals of four minutes of sidereal time. But, with the important exception of the Midheaven, house cusps also vary with latitude and the tables also show this variation at intervals of latitude. The tables give the variation at intervals of one degree of latitude, except between zero and 20 degrees, at which the variation is so small that intervals of five degrees are sufficient.

Obviously, because of these variations we cannot simply copy the cusps from the tables unless we are fortunate enough to have a birth which is both at an exact whole-number latitude and at a precise multiple of four minutes of sidereal time from 00:00:00! You do see cases in which one or the other is so close to exact that it is pointless to split hairs. For example, if you had a latitude of 30N00'04" or a sidereal time of 14:00:01, the adjustment would be so marginal as to be negligible; the cusp position would hardly differ from that shown in the table. But to have both almost exact would be a rare piece of good fortune. In most cases, we must make adjustments to reflect (1) the precise sidereal time and (2) the precise latitude.

To do this, we need two pieces of information and two calculations. The two pieces of information are (1) the earlier and later sidereal times in the intervals of four minutes which are closest to Jane's sidereal time; and (2) the higher and lower latitudes closest to her place of birth. The house cusps for these closest points are given in the tables of houses. Later, we will adjust them to match Jane's sidereal time and birth latitude, but first we will simply note them.

Information

CLOSEST EARLIER AND LATER SIDEREAL TIMES. In the tables of houses, find the two tables which most closely correspond to our calculated sidereal time. We need both the closest earlier time, and the closest later time. These closest times will be four minutes of sidereal time apart and our calculated sidereal time will be somewhere in that period of four minutes. Our calculated sidereal time is 14:04:57. From the appropriate page of the tables of houses you will see that the closest earlier time is 14:04:00 and the closest later time is 14:08:00. Note both on your worksheet.

CLOSEST HIGHER AND LOWER LATITUDES. Notice also that both tables give positions for latitudes between zero and 60 degrees in the Northern Hemisphere. The latitudes are listed between the second and third tables on each page of the book. The cusp of the Midheaven (tenth house) which varies only with sidereal time, and not with latitude, is shown at the very top of each table, just under the sidereal time. The eleventh through third houses, which vary both with sidereal time and latitude, each have their own columns. The fourth through the ninth houses, of course, will be exact opposites of the tenth through the third, so we need not worry about them for now. The latitude of Austin is 30N16'01", so the closest latitudes are 30 and 31. Note both on your worksheet.

Calculations

The two calculations we need to make are of two factors, called the sidereal time factor (STF) and the latitude factor (LF). The function of these factors is simply to adjust the house cusps shown in the tables of houses to reflect the exact sidereal time and latitude of birth. The final house cusps will fall somewhere between those for the closest sidereal times, and those for the closest latitudes, and these factors will pinpoint them exactly.

CALCULATION OF STF. To calculate the STF, find the interval in seconds between the calculated sidereal time and the closest earlier sidereal time, and divide the result by 240 (the number of seconds in the total interval of four minutes between the closest earlier and later times). Thus:

Calculated sidereal time   14:04:57
- Closest earlier time   14:04:00
Interval   00:00:57
STF = 57/240 = 0.2375

CALCULATION OF LF. The latitude factor is calculated by dividing the minutes and seconds of the birth latitude by 60 (the usual case between latitudes 21 and 60, where the closest higher and lower latitudes are one degree apart) or by 300 (in the unusual case between latitudes zero and 20, where they are five degrees apart). Of course, 60 is simply the number of minutes in one degree of latitude, and 300 the number of minutes in five degrees of latitude. Thus:

Minutes and seconds of latitude for Austin = 16′01″
Decimalized = 16.01666
LF = (16.01666 / 60) = 0.26694

Adjustments

Now, we will make our adjustments, using the information and factors we have just obtained. There are two adjustments to be made, the first to correspond with Jane's sidereal time, the second to correspond with her birth latitude. When we have made both adjustments, we will have the house cusps for Jane's natal chart.

SIDEREAL TIME ADJUSTMENT. To adjust for the precise calculated sidereal time, we go through the following steps. This is a lot simpler than it looks. Just be very methodical, and take your time.

Using the closest *lower* latitude:

1. Note the cusps for the closest later sidereal time.

2. Note the cusps for the closest earlier sidereal time.

Then, for each house in turn:

3. Calculate the distance between the two in minutes.

4. Multiply the distance by the STF. This gives us what is called the sidereal time correction.

5. Add the sidereal time correction to the minutes of the house cusp for the closest earlier time. If the total is more than 60, then, of course, you go into the next degree of the sign. (This is not the final cusp for this house, unless it is the tenth, because in all other cases, we must also adjust for latitude.)

Let's use the tenth house as an example.

At the closest lower latitude (30) -

The cusp for 14:08:00 is 4 Scorpio 16

The cusp for 14:04:00 is 3 Scorpio 13

The distance is one degree and three minutes, or 63 minutes.

Multiplying the distance (63 minutes) by the STF (0.2375) we arrive at 14.9625. This is the sidereal time correction.

Adding the sidereal time correction to the minutes of the earlier time cusp (13 + 14.9625) we get 27.9625. The cusp is, therefore, 3 Scorpio 27.9625, which rounds up to 3 Scorpio 28. As we are dealing with the tenth house, which needs no latitude correction, this will be the final cusp. Congratulations on completing our first definitive

Figure 7					
	11	**12**	**1(Asc)**	**2**	**3**
Later	0♐06	23♐02	16♑50	24♒26	2♈23
Earlier	29♏11	22♐08	15♑49	23♒14	11♈1
Distance (mins.)	55	54	61	72	72
x STF (0.2375) = sid. time correction	13.0625	12.825	14.4875	17.1	17.1
Cusp for earlier sid. time	29♏11	22♐08	15♑49	23♒14	1♈11
+ sid. time corr:	13.0625	12.825	14.4875	17.1	17.1
Cusps corrected for sidereal time	29824.062	22920.825	16003.4875	23-31.1	1128.1

calculation in Jane Doe's chart!

You can now do the same with each of the other houses, and the result will look something like Figure 7. For these other houses, however, we will not round up the result yet, because we still have to adjust for latitude.

Before moving on, notice that in the eleventh house, the cusp changed sign, not just degree, with the variation between the earlier and later sidereal time. Don't be confused by this. It is bound to happen sometimes when the earlier sidereal time cusp falls in the last degree of a sign. Remember that there are 30 degrees in each sign, and calculate the distance with this in mind. The simplest way to do this is to treat 0 Sagittarius 00 as if it were 30 Scorpio 00. When you arrive at your final cusp, simply remember that if the answer comes to 30 or more degrees of Scorpio, then the cusp is actually in zero degrees or more of Sagittarius. As it happens, in the case of Jane's chart, the cusp of this house will remain in Scorpio. This is because, after adjustment, the sidereal time was not late enough to take the cusp into Sagittarius.

LATITUDE ADJUSTMENT. For all houses except the tenth, we must now make an adjustment for latitude. The procedure for latitude adjustment is very similar to the sidereal time adjustment. But, because we are now concerned with latitude rather than sidereal time, we compare the cusps, not for different sidereal times, but for different latitudes. We work with the closest lower and the closest higher latitudes to the latitude of birth. As Austin is at latitude 30N16′01″, we will work with the cusps for latitudes 30 and 31. In calculating the latitude adjustment, we always take the cusps from the table for the closest *earlier* sidereal time (i.e., in this case, the table for 14:04:00.) as the basis for calculation.

In the table of cusps for the closest *earlier* sidereal time:

1. Note the cusps at the closest higher latitude.

2. Note the cusps at the closest lower latitude.

Then, for each house in turn:

3. Calculate the distance in minutes between the two.

4. Multiply the distance by the LF. The answer is called the latitude correction.

5. Add or subtract the latitude correction to or from the minutes of the cusp as already adjusted for sidereal time. You add if the higher latitude cusp is greater than the lower latitude cusp, subtract if the lower latitude cusp is greater. (This is in contrast to the sidereal time correction, which is always added.) If you look at the example below, you will see that, in the eleventh house, the cusp for the lower latitude (29 Scorpio 11) is greater than that for the higher (29 Scorpio 01) so, in this case, we subtract. The same is true of the twelfth, first and second houses. However, in the third house, the cusp for the higher latitude (1 Aries 12) is greater than that for the lower (1 Aries 11) so, in this case, we add.

6. Finally, round up or down to the nearest whole number.

Our worksheet will look something like Figure 8.

All that remains is to round the eleventh through the third house cusps up or down. Our cusps will then be:

Figure 8					
	11	**12**	**1 (Asc)**	**2**	**3**
Higher latitude	29♏01	21♐47	15♑14	22♒58	1♈12
Lower latitude	29♏11	22♐08	15♑49	23♒14	1♈11
Distance (mins.)	10	21	35	16	1
x LF (0.26694) = lat. corr.	2.6694	5.60574	9.3429	4.27104	0.26694
Cusp corrected For sid. time	29♏24.0625	2♐20.825	16♑03.4875	23-31.1	11♉8.1
+/- lat. corr.	- 2.6694	- 5.60574	- 9.3429	- 4.27104	+ 0.26694
Final cusp	29♏21.3931	22♐15.21926	15♑54.1446	23♒26.82896	1♈28.36694

Tenth—3 Scorpio 28

Eleventh—29 Scorpio 21

Twelfth—22 Sagittarius 15

First—15 Capricorn 54

Second—23 Aquarius 27

Third—1 Aries 28

And, of course, the remaining cusps will be their opposites:

Fourth—3 Taurus 28

Fifth—29 Taurus 21

Sixth—22 Gemini 15

Seventh—15 Cancer 54

Eighth—23 Leo 27

Ninth—1 Libra 28

BIRTHS IN THE SOUTHERN HEMISPHERE. The above cusps were calculated using a table of houses for latitudes in the Northern Hemisphere. If your birth was in the Southern Hemisphere, you follow exactly the same steps, but you now reverse the cusps. The tenth through third house cusps above would become those of the fourth through ninth houses, and *vice versa*.

Questions and Answers

Where do I find the House Cusps?

Answer: The house cusps are found in the tables of houses. The cusps all vary according to sidereal time, and all except the tenth also vary according to latitude. The tables give the cusps at intervals of four minutes of sidereal time, and whole degrees of latitude (except at extreme latitudes, where intervals of five degrees are given).

What is the formula for adjusting the cusps for sidereal time?

Answer:

1. Calculate the sidereal time factor (STF). STF = difference between the sidereal time at birth and the closest earlier sidereal time given in the tables, divided by 240.

2. Using the closest lower latitude, find the distance in minutes between the cusps for the closest earlier and later sidereal times. Multiply this by the STF.

3. Add the result to the minutes of the cusps for the earlier sidereal time.

4. Round off the cusp of the tenth house only to produce the final cusp.

What is the formula for adjusting the cusps for latitude?

Answer:

1. Calculate the latitude factor (LF). LF = minutes and seconds of latitude, divided by 60 (or if working with extreme latitudes in intervals of 5 degrees, by 300).

2. Using the closest earlier sidereal time, find the distance in minutes between the cusps for the higher and lower latitudes. Multiply this by the LF.

3. Add or subtract the result to or from the minutes of the cusps as already adjusted for sidereal time. Add if the cusp for the higher latitude is greater than that for the lower latitude. Subtract if the cusp for the lower latitude is greater.

What is the formula for producing the final house cusps?

Answer:

1. Round off to the nearest minute to produce the final cusps.

2. For Southern Hemisphere births, reverse the cusps, so that the tenth through the third become those of the fourth through the ninth, and *vice versa*.

Chapter 5

Calculating the Planetary Positions

The planetary positions are calculated from the ephemeris. It is a relatively straightforward procedure, provided you remember that we are using a midnight Greenwich ephemeris. The planetary positions are always shown as at midnight GMT on each day. (Because the Moon is so swift, some ephemerides also give its noon position, but for consistency we will work with the midnight position.) Therefore, we must always use the GMT birth time, and we must always use the Greenwich birth date, which, you will recall, may differ from the American birth date if the birth took place in the evening in the United States.

The positions of the Sun and Moon are given in three columns—degrees, minutes and seconds. The positions of the other planets are given only in degrees and minutes, although the minutes are decimalized for calculating seconds if desired. However, it is unnecessary to do this for normal purposes. The practice is simply to round up or down to the nearest minute. The ephemeris also tells us whether a planet was direct or retrograde at the time of birth—an important piece of information. Retrograde is indicated by the letter "R."

Not all ephemerides include Chiron, but some give its position on a monthly basis in the footnotes. We will deal separately with Chiron after calculating the other planetary positions.

Please look again at the page of the ephemeris for May 1945. What we are going to do is simply this:

1. Decimalize the GMT birth time. Our GMT birth time is 04:42:00, which, when decimalized, becomes 4.7.

2. Note the positions of each planet at midnight GMT on the Greenwich birth date. As we have seen, Jane's Greenwich birth date is May 21, 1945, not May 20.

3. Note the positions at midnight GMT on the following day (May 22).

4. Calculate the total distance traveled by each planet during that period of 24 hours.

5. Calculate the distance traveled by each planet between midnight GMT on the birth date and the GMT birth time. This is done by dividing the total distance of travel by 24, and multiplying the result by the number of hours between midnight and the GMT birth time, in our case, 4.7. So, we will divide by 24 and multiply by 4.7. This will give us the distance actually travelled by each planet between midnight and the time of birth. If you are using the a.m./p.m. system, be sure you know whether the birth is a.m. or p.m. The interval of a 4 a.m. birth from midnight is four hours; the interval of a 4 p.m. birth is 16 hours!

5. Lastly, we will calculate the planetary position at the time of birth by adding the actual distance travelled to the position at midnight on the birth date, except when the planet is retrograde, in which case we subtract the ac-

tual distance traveled from the position at midnight. To do this addition or subtraction, convert the decimals back into minutes and, in the case of the Sun and Moon, seconds.

Let's take an example, using the Sun. As in our house cusp calculations, we have an example of a potential sign change. Deal with it in exactly the same way. Sign changes are not uncommon, especially with the Moon, which takes only about 29 days to travel through the zodiac.

Position at midnight GMT on May 21, 1945:	29 ♉ 34 21
Position at midnight on following day:	00 ♊ 32 02
Distance traveled in 24 hours:	00 57 41
Distance decimalized = 57.68333 minutes	
Actual travel = (57.68333 / 24) x 4.7 = 11.29631 minutes	
Converted to minutes and seconds = 11:18	
Position at midnight GMT on May 21, 1945:	29 ♉ 34 21
+ distance travelled at birth time:	11 18
Position of Sun	29 ♉ 45 39

So, the Sun did not quite make it into Gemini. The remaining planetary positions are calculated in the same way. So are the positions of the nodes of the Moon. Because of the swiftness of the Moon, the distance of travel is much greater than those of the other planets, and you can either work in degrees, minutes and seconds, or convert the degrees to minutes, and treat her the same way as the others. Our worksheet might look something like Figures 9 through 12.

In copying these positions on to the wheel, you can, of course, round the seconds and decimals up or down to the nearest whole minute.

You will already know that the outer planets are very slow moving, and, for almost all purposes, you can simply take the midnight position on the birthdate or the following day, whichever is closer to your birth time. However, for the sake of completeness, we will calculate them in the same way but only to one decimal point. We will do the same with the North Node. The South Node, of course, is exactly opposite and need not be calculated separately.

In the examples in Figures 10 and 11, please look carefully at the calculation for Neptune and the North Node, which were retrograde at the time of Jane's birth. Also note that where there is no possible change of sign, the sign can be omitted except in the first and last lines, but it is safer always to include the retrograde abbreviation.

The South Node, of course, will be at 10001R. The positions given for the Nodes in the ephemeris are for the true nodes. The values for the mean nodes are shown in the footnotes.

CHIRON. The ephemeris gives positions for Chiron only on the first day of each month. There are more detailed ephemerides available, such as that in Melanie Reinhart's *Chiron and the Healing Journey*, which gives positions at intervals of 10 days. However, the following calculation will suffice for all normal purposes. It is essentially the same as the other planetary calculations. Note the position of Chiron on the first day of the month of birth and the first day of the following month. Calculate the distance traveled in the month. Divide the distance by the number of days in the month, and multiply by the number of the day of birth at Greenwich. The calculation for Jane's Chiron will look like Figure 12.

Figure 9				
	☽	☿	♀	♂
Position Midnight May 21	22♍41:36	5♉41.9	20♈41.4	13♈52.4
Position Midnight May 22	4♎35:49	7♉07.0	21♈09.9	14♈37.9
Distance 24 hours	11 54:13	1 25.1	28.5	45.5
Actual travel				
(distance/24) x 4.7 =	2 19:52	16.66	5.58	8.91
Position Midnight May 21	22♍41:36	5♉41.9	20♈41.4	13♈52.4
+ Travel	2 19:52	16.66	5.58	8.91
Position	25♍01:28	5♉58.56	20♈46.38	14♈01.31

Figure 10

	♃	♄	♅	♆
Position Midnight May 21	17♍35.1	8♋35.2	12♊23.7	3♋8.8R
Position Midnight May 22	17　36.3	8　41.9	12　27.2	3　48.1R
Distance 24 hours	1.2	6.7	3.5	0.7
Actual travel				
(distance / 24) x 4.7 =	0.2	1.3	0.6	0.1
Position Midnight May 21	17　35.1	8　35.2	12　23.7	3　48.8R
+/- travel	+　0.2	+　1.3	+　0.6	-　0.1
Position	17♍35.3	8♋36.5	12♊24.3	3♋8.7R

Figure 11

	♀	☊
Position May 21	8♌06.8	10♋0.9R
Position May 22	8　7.6	9　56.7R
Distance 24 hours:	0.8	4.2
Actual travel		
(Distance/24) x 4.7 =	0.1	0.8
Position May 21	8　6.8	10　0.9R
+/- actual travel	+　0.1	-　0.8
Position	8♌6.9	10♋0.1R

Figure 12

Position on May 1, 1945	27♍29.9R
Position on June 1	26　59.8D
Distance in month	30.1
Actual travel	
(Distance/31) x 21 =	20.4
Position on May 1	27　29.9R
- actual travel	20.4
Position	27♍09.5R

At some point in the month, Chiron went direct. To find out exactly when (it was actually on May 25) you would need to consult a more detailed Chiron ephemeris such as that in Melanie Reinhart's book. This will tell you whether Chiron was direct or retrograde on the date of birth. When using a monthly ephemeris, there will be some degree of inaccuracy.

Questions and Answers

How do I find the planetary positions?

Answer: The positions for midnight GMT on a daily basis are given in the ephemeris. Make sure you know whether the birth time has changed the date of birth, when expressed in GMT. Because we are using a Greenwich midnight ephemeris, it is essential to use the correct GMT birth date and birth time when calculating the planetary positions.

What is the formula for calculating planetary positions?

Answer:

1. Note position of planet at midnight on Greenwich birth date. Note position 24 hours later. Find the travel in 24-hour period.

2. Divide travel by 24, and multiply by interval between midnight on birth date and birth time (birth time in 24-hour clock, decimalized).

3. Add result to earlier position (if direct) or subtract from earlier position (if retrograde).

4. Round off to nearest minute.

Chapter 6

Calculating the Part of Fortune and the Part of Spirit

Traditional astrology makes use of two points in space known as the Part of Fortune and the Part of Spirit. There are several other such parts, which have formulae similar to these two. These parts are often referred to as Arabic Parts, though historical evidence shows that they derive from the older Hellenistic astrology. The formulae consist of taking the distance between two planets or points, and adding that distance to the Ascendant. In modern astrology, it has become usual to calculate the Part of Fortune using the formula (Asc + Moon) - Sun, and the Part of Spirit using the formula (Asc + Sun) - Moon. However, it is clear from a review of traditional sources that this is a modern simplification. The true rule is that the first formula shown above gives the Part of Fortune for diurnal charts, and the Part of Spirit for nocturnal charts; the second formula gives the Part of Fortune for nocturnal charts, and the Part of Spirit for diurnal charts. A diurnal chart is defined as being one in which the Sun is placed above the horizon (in houses seven through twelve) and a nocturnal chart as one in which the Sun is placed below the horizon (in houses one through six). Whether a chart is diurnal or nocturnal cannot be ascertained solely by reference to the time of birth, even though we speak loosely of a person being born "during the daytime" or "at night." It is a function of the actual house position of the Sun. If the birth occurred at a time close to sunrise or sunset, it will not be clear whether the Sun falls above or below the horizon until the cusps are calculated precisely.

As an example, let us use the first formula. We take the position of the Ascendant, add the position of the Moon, and then deduct the position of the Sun. There are two equally good methods of doing this, both quite simple. Which you choose is simply a matter of preference.

The Sign Method

The sign method consists of working in three columns: signs, degrees and minutes. If you use this method, the only thing to remember is that the maximum number for each column is different. There are 12 signs; there are 30 degrees in each sign; there are 60 minutes in each degree. If you arrive at a number greater than 12 in the sign column, deduct 12. The number which goes in the sign column is the number of the sign in the zodiac, for example Aries will be 01, Taurus will be 02, and so on. So, in Jane's case:

	Sign	Degrees	Minutes
Ascendant (15♈54)	10	15	54
+ Moon (25♍01)	06	25	01
	17	10	55

	- Sun		
(29♉45)	<u>02</u>	<u>29</u>	<u>45</u>
	14	11	10
Deduct 12	<u>12</u>	<u>00</u>	<u>00</u>
Result:	02	11	10

The second sign of the zodiac is Taurus, so the position is 11 Taurus 10. Because Jane's chart is nocturnal (the Sun is in the fifth house) this position will be that of the Part of Spirit.

The Distance Method

The distance method consists of expressing the positions of the Ascendant, Moon and Sun in terms of the number of degrees their positions are from a starting point of 0 Aries 00. Of course, zero degrees of each successive sign is 30 degrees further from 0 Aries 00. So, 0 Taurus 00 is 30 degrees away, 0 Gemini 00 is 60 degrees, and so on. In our case, the Ascendant is 15 Capricorn 54. 0 Capricorn 00 is 270 degrees from 0 Aries 00. Add to this the further 15 degrees and 54 minutes, and the value for the Ascendant is 285:54. Do the same with the Sun and Moon. In the case of the Sun, 0 Taurus 00 is 30 degrees from 0 Aries 00. Add the remaining 29 degrees, 45 minutes, and you will arrive at a value of 59:45. In the case of the Moon, 0 Virgo 00 is 150 degrees from 0 Aries 00. Add the remaining 25:01, and the value is 175:01. Actually, all we are doing here is using two columns instead of three. In this method, the total can never exceed 360 degrees (12 signs x 30 degrees) so if the total is greater, deduct 360. Our calculation will now look like this.

Ascendant	285:54
+ Moon	<u>175:01</u>
	460:55
- Sun	<u>59:45</u>
	401:10
Deduct 360	<u>360:00</u>
Result	41:10

If we add 41:10 to 0 Aries 00, we arrive at the same position, namely 11 Taurus 10.

As this is a nocturnal chart, the second formula, (Asc + Sun) - Moon, will give us the Part of Fortune. Using both methods demonstrated above, we have:

Ascendant	10 15 54	285 54
+ Sun	<u>02 29 45</u>	<u>59 45</u>
	13 15 39	345 39
-Moon	<u>06 25 01</u>	<u>175 01</u>
Result	06 20 38	170 38

By either method, we arrive at a position of 20 Virgo 38.

Chapter 7

Detecting and Correcting Errors

There are two ways to deal with the possibility of errors in calculation. Both are important. Obviously, one is to check the accuracy of the entire work once it is completed. If you have a computer calculation program, it is quite easy to do this. Your results may differ marginally from those of the computer, because the computer works with higher degrees of mathematical accuracy, but you should arrive at the same figures within a minute or so in most cases. The values for the Nodes and Chiron may be a little farther off. (At the end of this chapter is Jane Doe's chart calculated by computer program. From this, we see that we have been successful in constructing her chart accurately.) If you do not have a computer, all you can do is check and recheck your work, or have someone else do so.

The second way is to make "ballpark" checks as you go along, in the hope of an early warning of something going wrong. Fortunately, there is a definite connection between certain procedural errors (such as miscalculation, mixing up the steps in the calculations, or working with inaccurate data) and a resulting error in a predictable area, such as house cusps or planetary positions. By keeping an intelligent eye on the emerging results during your work, you will soon learn to guess pretty well what is going wrong, if anything is. This will save much time and wasted effort. We now want to show you some correlations between procedural errors and result errors, and some useful methods of making ballpark checks.

Until you have had considerable practice, you will find that you make mistakes quite frequently. Keep using the pencil and eraser! Do not be discouraged. Everyone has the same experience. Fortunately, a mistake does not usually mean that you have to do everything again. Let's begin with a short list of very common correlations. Of course, it is not exhaustive. Result errors can be caused by arithmetical errors at any stage. But the following are very common sources of error.

Incorrect Result	Possible Error
House cusps	Incorrect latitude
	Incorrect STF or LF
	Incorrect sidereal time, which could be:
	Failure to deduct for DT/WT
	Incorrect longitude correction
	Incorrect TLT, which could be:
	Error in adding v. subtracting time
	zone correction
	If using a.m./p.m. clock, failing to add
	12 hours for p.m. birth for midnight-TLT interval

Planetary positions	Failure to deduct for DT/WT
	Incorrect GMT birth time
	Incorrect GMT birth date
	(Was birth p.m. in U.S.?)

Next, we want to give you some more specific guidelines which will serve you well either during the calculation process, or in investigating errors. They should enable you to anticipate the answers you should be getting to a reasonable approximation. If your answers are dramatically different from the approximation, it would be a good idea to check that stage of your work before proceeding further. This is not meant to intimidate you! It is simply to let you know the magnitude of error in the results associated with procedural errors of different kinds. Often, this knowledge can be very useful—a result error of a certain predictable magnitude often points straight to the procedural error, enabling you to make a simple and quick correction.

Failure to Deduct for DT/WT

This will result in a + 1 hour error in the calculation of TLT and Greenwich birth time. Therefore:

1. The calculated sidereal time will be in error by plus one hour of sidereal time. This will give an error in the house cusps of about 15 degrees. For example, in Jane's chart, the Midheaven for the closest earlier sidereal time (14:04:00) was 3 Scorpio 13. But the midheaven for an incorrect closest earlier sidereal time of 15:04:00 would be 18 Scorpio 28. If your cusps are about 15 degrees off, this could be the reason. This is a major error, resulting, among other things in a potentially incorrect rising sign, and incorrect house cusps throughout the chart.

2. The Greenwich birth time equivalent will also be in error by plus one hour. This will result in an error of $\frac{1}{24}$ in the actual travel of the planets from the midnight position, and therefore, will produce incorrect planetary positions. Fortunately, except in the case of the Moon, the error is minimal.

Error in Adding v. Subtracting Longitude Correction

This will produce an error in the calculated sidereal time of up to eight minutes either plus or minus. The longitude correction never exceeds two minutes, but an error in adding instead of subtracting, or *vice versa*, will produce an error of double the longitude correction, or up to four minutes of sidereal time. This will result in an error of up to two degrees in the house cusps. This may be a serious error, depending on sign changes, and will always produce incorrect house cusps.

Failure to Add Acceleration

This will produce a similar error in the calculated sidereal time, of up to 3:59:59 of sidereal time. This may result in an error of up to 1 degree in the house cusps. There will be an error in the final house cusps, as in the case of the longitude correction error. Both errors together, of course, increase the inaccuracy.

Miscalculation of Interval of TLT-Previous Midnight

As we have seen, this error is most likely to occur when you are using an a.m./p.m. clock and you have an afternoon birth. If the birth took place at a TLT of 10:00 p.m., a common error is to put down 10 hours as the interval between TLT and the previous midnight. Of course, this is incorrect. 10:00 a.m. would be an interval of 10 hours, but 10:00 p.m. is an interval of 22 hours. This is a massive error, which will give an inaccuracy of more or less 180 degrees in the positions of the house cusps.

Addition v. Subtraction of Latitude Correction

Unlike the sidereal time correction, which is always added, the latitude correction is either added or subtracted, according to the relative size of the cusps for the closest lower and higher latitude. The method for choosing addition or subtraction is covered in the text. Choosing the wrong procedure here can result in an error in the final house cusp of double the longitude correction. This can be anything from a few minutes to a full degree, and could result in a sign change.

Finally, we want to offer a few ways of making "ballpark checks" of your emerging house cusp and planetary position data, as you go along.

Methods for Making A Ballpark Check of House Cusps

It is useful to be able to make a ballpark check of the emerging house cusps in your work in progress, as you go along. Once you get the feel of what you are doing, you will begin to see whether the emerging house cusp positions are "in the ballpark," and, if not, you will be alerted to the need to review your calculations. This awareness can save a lot of time and wasted effort. The following methods may help.

1. The emerging cusp will be at a point between the cusps for the closest earlier and closest later sidereal time. Check that this point is approximately proportional to the point of the calculated sidereal time between the earlier and later times. For example, assume that the cusp of the eleventh house is 28 Libra 00 at sidereal time 11:44:00, and 29 Libra 03 at sidereal time 11:48:00. Assume further that your calculated sidereal time is 11:46:00. As the calculated sidereal time is half way between the closest earlier and later sidereal times, the cusp, as corrected for sidereal time only, should be about half way between the two cusps, i.e. at about 28 Libra 31.

2. The emerging cusp will also be at a point between the cusps for the closest higher and lower latitudes. Similarly, check that this point is approximately proportional to the point of the birth latitude between the closest higher and lower latitudes. For example, assume that the cusp of the eleventh house at sidereal time 11:44:00 is 26 Libra 01 at latitude 29, and 25 Libra 56 at latitude 30. Assume further that the birth latitude is 29N45'02. As the birth latitude is approximately three quarters of the way from latitude 29 to latitude 30, the emerging cusp, as corrected for latitude only, should be about three quarters of the way towards latitude 30 from latitude 29, which would be about 25 Libra 57/58.

Bear in mind that the above two tests are to check the accuracy of the sidereal time and latitude adjustments only. The final cusp is calculated using both adjustments. However, if you have made both adjustments correctly, you are bound to reach the correct final position.

3. As a general rule, a person born between 06:00:00 and 08:00:00 (6:00 and 8:00 a.m.) will have his or her Sun sign on the Ascendant. The signs will then rotate through the Ascendant at the rate of one sign per two hours. Therefore, in general, a person born with Sun in Aries between 06:00:00 and 08:00:00 will have Aries rising; the same person born between 08:00:00 and 10:00:00 will have Taurus rising; between 10:00:00 and 12:00:00, Gemini rising; and so on. We must emphasize that this is only an approximate test. For one thing, it does not always work, because a combination of latitude and late degrees of a sign on the cusp can throw it off. And, even when it does work, it merely tells you what sign, not what degree, is on the Ascendant, and so is inadequate for accurate calculation. Nonetheless, it is valuable as a guide, because it will be accurate within one sign either way. If your emerging Ascendant is inaccurate, judged by this test—especially, of course, if it is off by more than one sign—it is worth reviewing your house cusp calculations (all of them, not just for the Ascendant).

Methods for Making Ballpark Checks of Planetary Positions

You are unlikely to have many problems in this area, unless you select an incorrect GMT birth date or time. Any problems which do arise will be with the inner planets. The outer planets move so little in the course of 24 hours, that any substantial error is almost impossible, and you will soon be able to calculate their positions mentally with little effort. The following observations may help in making a ballpark assessment of your emerging inner planet positions during your work in progress.

CHART POSITION OF THE SUN. One revolution of the zodiacal wheel takes 24 hours—two hours per sign, or four minutes per degree. Because we define 24 hours as being the time the Sun takes to make one complete revolution about the ecliptic, it is possible to check the position of the Sun in the chart in ballpark terms by reference to the time of birth. Like the method for checking the Ascendant, this method is accurate only in general terms, but it is nonetheless useful in detecting gross errors. For a birth within an hour or two either way of 6:00 a.m., the Sun will be in the general area of the Ascendant, either the twelfth or first house; for a birth within an hour or two of midday, in the general area of the Midheaven (ninth or tenth house); for a birth within an hour or two of 6:00 p.m., in the general area of the Descendant (sixth or seventh house); and, for a birth within an hour or two of midnight, in the general area of the Nadir (third or fourth house). If the emerging position of the Sun differs materially from these guidelines, review your calculation.

CHART POSITION OF MERCURY AND VENUS. Mercury will never be more than about 28 degrees from the Sun. Venus will never be more than about 48 degrees from the Sun. If your calculations have produced significantly greater distances, they are in error. Mercury and Venus will frequently be in the same sign as the Sun, but this will not necessarily be the case. They may also frequently be in the same house, but again, not necessarily so.

DIURNAL MOTION. Another useful indicator for the Sun, the Moon, and the inner planets, is the range of travel of each within a 24-hour period, known as the diurnal motion of the planet. The diurnal motion of the planets is not absolutely consistent from day to day, but varies to a relatively small degree and within a predictable range. With the exception of the Sun and the Moon, all the planets have periods of retrograde motion. On approach to retrograde motion, the planet's diurnal motion will slow down until it becomes stationary, and then it will gradually pick up speed in retrograde motion. On emergence from retrograde, the planet will slow again, move into direct motion, and gradually pick up speed, until its maximum diurnal motion is achieved. If you are aware of all this, it will enable you to check your ballpark position quickly and accurately. You will always have an accurate general sense of the range of travel to be anticipated within any given period of 24 hours, which makes it fairly easy to come to a ballpark position within that range, based on the birth time. The following observations may prove useful.

The Sun. The diurnal motion of the Sun is in the range 0:57:12 to 1:01:10 (degrees, minutes and seconds). By definition, the Sun orbits the zodiac (360 degrees) in one year (or 365 days). Therefore, it is obvious that the diurnal motion of the Sun must be in the ballpark of one degree per day. Its average diurnal motion is about 00:59:08.

The Moon. The Moon is, of course, the swiftest-moving planet of all. Her diurnal motion is, therefore, far greater than that of any other planet. Whereas, with the other planets, we are usually dealing with minutes, or at most between one and two degrees, the Moon travels a number of degrees in any period of 24 hours, changing signs every two or three days. The Moon orbits the zodiac in approximately 29 days. Her diurnal motion is in the range 11:50:00 to 15:18:00, with an average of 13:10:36. Calculations involving the Moon, although no more difficult than those involving any other planet, are more critical and prone to greater degrees of error. They should always be checked carefully.

Mercury. Mercury orbits the zodiac in about 88 days, so that it orbits a little more than four times per year. However, its direct diurnal motion is nothing like the four plus degrees suggested by the orbital period, because Mercury goes retrograde three times each year, for a period of about two weeks each time. Mercury's average diurnal motion is approximately 1:23:00.

Venus. Venus orbits the zodiac in about 224.5 days, about 1.6 times per year. It has periods of retrograde motion, which are far less frequent than those of Mercury. Its average diurnal motion is about 1:12:00.

Mars and the outer planets. The remaining planets rarely cause difficulties. Although the outer planets (especially Chiron) have rather elliptical orbits, and although they all have prolonged periods of retrograde motion, their diurnal motion is so small that any variation within a period of 24 hours is insignificant for the purposes of a ballpark check. The following table should be a sufficient guide, as long as you remember that all the figures given are subject to some small variation.

Planet	Orbital period	Normal direct diurnal motion
Mars	22 months	Up to about 45 minutes
Jupiter	12 years	Up to about 14 minutes
Saturn	29 years	Up to about 8 minutes
Chiron	51 years	Up to about 5 minutes
Uranus	84 years	Less than 4 minutes
Neptune	165 years	Less than 3 minutes
Pluto	248 years	Up to about 2 minutes

Figure 13 is the natal chart for Jane Doe with which you can compare our manual calculations.

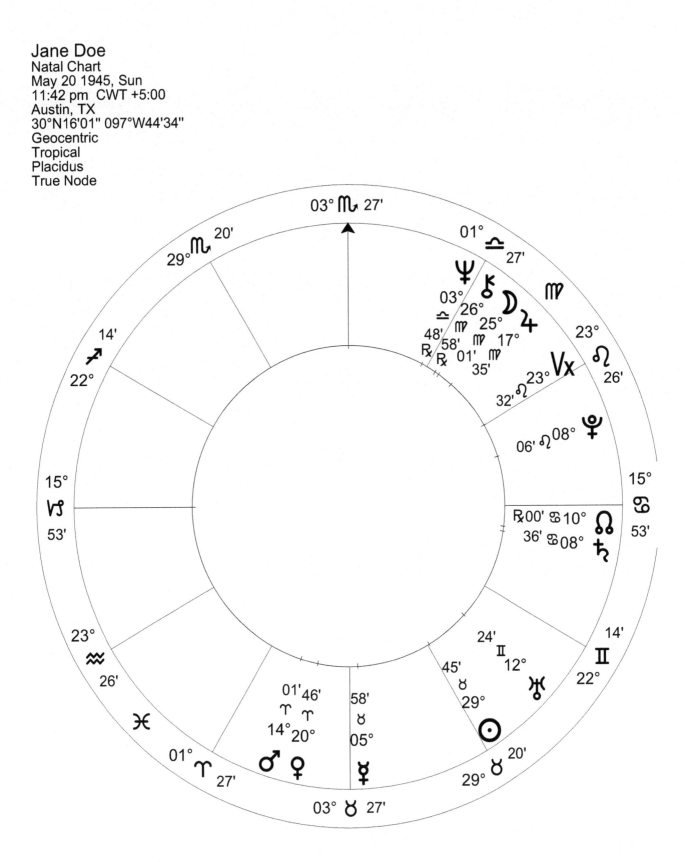

Figure 13

Chapter 8

Copying the Data
to the Blank Wheel

All that remains is to copy the data you have calculated to a blank wheel. Some people make a real work of art of this, and some hand drawn charts could be exhibited in an art museum. But if you are reading this with undisguised envy, and have a limited artistic ability, don't panic. An acceptable standard is that the chart should be basically legible. Remember that the Ascendant is always drawn on the left (east) side of the chart, and the houses are then indicated counterclockwise around the wheel, in relation to the ascending degree.

Some blank wheels have the house cusps predrawn at even distances, so that the relative size of the houses does not appear. This is fine if you are using an equal house system, but if using Placidus or another quadrant house system, a wheel without predrawn house cusps, but graduated into 360 degrees, is preferable. You then draw the cusps yourself. If you do this, the convention is that, if the Ascendant is in the range zero to 15 degrees of the sign, you position the Ascendant the appropriate number of degrees down from the horizontal, so that the Ascendant-Descendant axis appears to slope upwards from left to right. If the Ascendant is in the range of 16 to 29 degrees of the sign, you position the Ascendant up from the horizontal, so that the axis slopes downwards from left to right. We recommend that you distinguish the Ascendant and the Midheaven by using red ink, the other house cusps being drawn in black. If you are using a system of equal houses from the Ascendant, remember that the Midheaven will be separate from the cusp of the tenth house, so indicate it separately.

The house cusps should always be written on the outside of the wheel. The presence of intercepted signs should also be indicated on the perimeter by including the glyph between two vertical lines. The planetary positions are written inside the wheel, and should be indicated in black.

Practice varies as to the direction in which the planetary positions should be written. It is universally agreed that the planetary positions should be written inside the wheel. It is also agreed that the planetary glyphs should be written on the perimeter, and that the degrees and minutes of position should "sandwich" the sign glyph, i.e. the sign glyph goes in the middle. But there is some variation as to how to position the degrees and minutes. Some astrologers and computer programs always write the positions towards the center of the wheel, so that the degree is always outside the planetary glyph. This has the merit of consistency, but involves having to read from right to left on the west (right-hand) side of the wheel. If you find this awkward, an equally acceptable convention is to write left-to-right or top-to bottom, whichever is easier. You will find that left-to-right usually works best in the twelfth, first, sixth and seventh houses, and top-to-bottom in the others, but this will vary somewhat with the relative size of the houses, and the angle of the Ascendant-Descendant axis. The retrograde symbol is always written next to the minutes of the position.

It is worth making a list of what has to go in each house before you start copying. Sometimes, a particular house gets pretty crowded, and you may need to write smaller in that house to fit everything in. It is very frustrating to fill a house from cusp to cusp and then find you still have Pluto to accommodate. Unless you are working in pencil, you may have to start again!

If you wish, you can indicate aspects. This is done using colored lines joining the aspected planets or points, and the convention is to use green for conjunctions and sextiles, blue for trines, red for squares and oppositions, and any distinguishable color for minor aspects. We would advise caution in the number of aspects you indicate, particularly when it comes to minor aspects, because an undue proliferation of lines can make the chart very difficult to read. Many astrologers take the sensible course of indicating major patterns, such as grand trines and T-squares, and perhaps one or two other especially significant aspects.

As we indicated earlier, do not be dismayed if there is a discrepancy of about one minute either way between your manual calculation and the computer program's calculation. This is to be expected, especially when dealing with the Nodes and with Chiron if you are using only the monthly positions given in the ephemeris. However, even in these cases, a discrepancy of more than two minutes warrants a revision of your calculations.

Complete the exercise by copying the data to your blank wheel. After you have finished, check it against the one shown below. This was drawn using a graduated wheel without predrawn house cusps, and using the convention of writing left-to-right, top-to-bottom.

Now that you know how to do it, try constructing the four charts in the practice exercise section. You will find the necessary pages from the ephemeris and tables of houses provided. The worksheets and finished charts are to be found in the answer section. And, after you have finished those charts, do as many as you can. Just as with every skill in life, there is no substitute for practice. When you begin, you may find yourself taking up to two hours to complete a chart, but after lots of practice, the time will come down to about 45 minutes.

Most of all, enjoy, and learn to love the feel of an emerging chart.

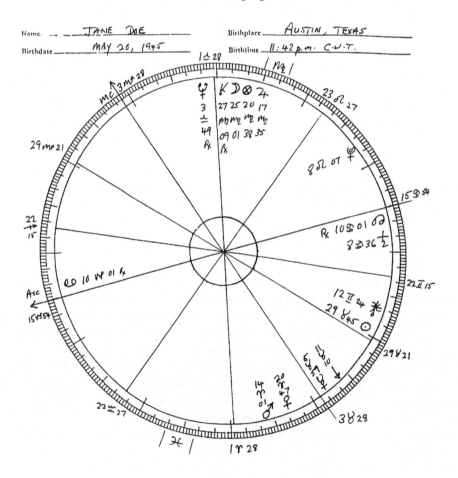

Chapter 9

What Do I Do Now?

Getting in Touch with the Chart

Why have we studied all this math, to arrive at a natal chart, which our computers could have accomplished in much less time? It's a real question, and one which deserves a good answer. Chart construction is a means to an end. The end is the understanding of the natal chart of a human being, an understanding which can bring real benefit to that human being's life, and which you, as an astrologer, can provide.

Once you have studied this book, and had a little practice, you will find that you can erect a natal chart without too much difficulty. Practice is the key here. Take every opportunity you can to calculate charts by hand. Erect charts for everyone you can think of, family, friends, the President, anybody. If you run out of real people, invent some birth data, just as we did with Jane Doe. The more often you repeat the procedure, the easier and faster it will become. It's really not as difficult as it may seem, once you get the hang of it.

But, once you have the birth chart in front of you, astrology can seem a little overwhelming. The chart you've constructed contains signs, planets, houses, aspects and lunar Nodes. If you survey the astrological literature, it seems there's so much to think about. You'll read about the Part of Fortune, the Part of Spirit, asteroids, the Vertex, fixed stars . . . you get the idea! Sometimes, the complexity of astrology can indeed seem daunting, confusing students to the point where they feel like giving up. "There's so much to it! I'll never learn it all! I'll never be able to read a chart." Everyone who studies astrology has felt this kind of frustration at one time or another. If you're reading this book, you may be feeling some frustration right now. If you have been practicing chart construction, the eraser on your pencil may have been worn away to almost nothing by constant use.

So, here are a few words of richly-deserved comfort and encouragement. The process of calculating a natal chart begins the process of understanding on a subtle but very real level. Just by going through the steps, and watching the chart emerge, house by house, planet by planet, you will learn more than you realize about the subject. One of the most valuable things you can do as an astrologer is simply to spend time looking at the chart, taking in its shape, its patterns, its symmetrical symbolism. This simple act of observation will allow the chart to begin to open itself up to you.

When looking at a computer-generated chart, you may not be very impressed with the symmetrical symbolism of the chart. For all their accuracy, computer charts are not aesthetically stimulating or visually personal. This is why we urged you in the previous section to draw your charts by hand. Because you are reading this book, we assume that you have learned or intend to learn to do the math of chart construction. But whether you prepare the calculations or use a computer, draw the chart by hand. The very act of transposing astrological information to a page—of using a pen, feeling the paper, or creating the slant and flow of the ancient glyphs, of absorbing the feel of the planetary placements and relationships as you draw them—contributes to your opportunity to make contact with the chart. It creates a perceptual link between yourself and the symbolism you are attempting to interpret.

The chart does emerge as you prepare it. It comes to life as a symbol, because you are creating it. It comes to birth through your preparation of its body, which is the calculation. It derives its spirit through your artistry in interpretation, in perceiving its potential as symbolism. Making creative, emotional and intuitive contact with the chart by actually drawing it by hand is one of the strongest and most powerful steps you can take in forging a personal link with the symbol you will be interpreting.

Essentially, astrology is interpretation. If you have a thirst for astrology, if it stirs some passion in you, if it interests you, excites you, makes you think in a new way, then astrology is for you. So, set aside any frustration which arises from your struggle with the math, and concentrate on astrology. Astrology is really very straightforward in its basics. All you really need to understand in order to read a natal chart are the signs, the planets and the houses. Knowing how to interpret these three basic ingredients will give you hours of insight into any chart.

After you've mastered these basics, you will have the right foundation to learn about aspects, transits and progressions. And, in time, you may discover that all the rest of the information an astrologer uses or explores isn't really as confusing as it first seems. Nor is it absolutely essential to the practice of good astrology. It's a rare astrologer who incorporates all sorts of complicated, unusual information into his or her everyday work. In fact, the opposite is true. Most astrologers strive for simplicity.

Always try to make simplicity a watchword. If you are stumped by a set of factors in a chart, and you feel the swirl of confusion building, pull yourself back to center by whispering the word "simplicity" to yourself. What is the core of the information you are trying to analyze? What is the basic principle at work?

For example, if you are trying to analyze a grand trine involving two single planets and one conjunction, you can easily become overwhelmed if you're looking at the big picture. What does Sun trine Jupiter trine a Mars-Saturn conjunction mean? What about adding the sign placements and houses? Makes you feel like running for cover, doesn't it?

But what is at the core of the information you're trying to analyze? Basically, you're looking at a series of trines. What is the nature of a trine aspect? It represents a harmonious relationship between two planets, creating an ease between the flow of planetary drives. It makes expressing those drives a bit easier, removes some of the potential challenge, and also some of the potential drives, which might be associated with those planets.

In the example we gave, you're basically looking at trines—trines involving the Sun, Jupiter, Mars and Saturn. So, all of these planets will have a bit of "smoothness" to their expression. Aha! This person may have a lot of confidence; maybe that Mars-Saturn conjunction is made a bit easier by its involvement in the grand trine. There is a feeling that things will always work out from this person's point of view. Things may happen which soften the blows of life. Perhaps sometimes he or she may take things too easy. Trines, trines, trines.

Now look at the signs. What elements are involved? Remember, that will give you the basic quality of the signs, and we're looking for simplicity here. Is the configuration in fire, earth, air, or water? Look at the houses in the same way. What meaning do they contribute? The result will be the basic core of what the grand trine is all about.

You can fill in more detailed observations later if you feel like it. For now, because you've simplified, you have made contact with the heart of the information. And, hopefully, you've avoided most of the overwhelming stress and panic that trying to process so much information may initially trigger.

The Feel of the Chart

After you have drawn the chart, take some time and just absorb the symbol itself, its pattern, the way it is laid out. That very shaping will tell you a lot about the chart. It's a very simple way to begin to get the general "feel" of the way in which the chart and, therefore, the individual it represents, are expressed. Remember that on the most basic level a chart is a symbol. A symbol speaks as much to the subconscious as it does to the conscious, logical mind. By drawing the chart yourself and by taking the time simply to perceive and digest the chart on emotional and intuitive levels instead of rushing it to make "sensible" delineations, you give yourself the chance to absorb the feel of the chart on a subliminal level, to let its symbolism speak to you.

Once you sense that you have the feel, look at the elemental balance of the chart. How are the planets distributed among the signs by element? For example, if there is only one planet in an earth sign but that planet happens to be ruler of the Ascendant, this merits attention. Even if there are quite a few more planets in other elements, the chart ruler in earth gives equal importance to earth in that chart. Obviously, if there are five planets in a particular element, you should pay attention to that regardless of what the five planets are. But if a planet which is exceptionally strong by placement is all alone in an element, that should be noted too. In other words, quality as well as quantity counts when it comes to the elements.

Taking note of the elemental placements of the planets by sign and then by house gives a wonderful feel for the rudimentary energies of the chart. What are the important drives and orientations? The elements tell us a lot about them. Once again, we are not talking primarily about conscious deductions. Elementary energy is usually highly instinctive, highly subconscious. Elements represent basic temperamental qualities: fire is spirit; earth is sensuality; air is intellect; water is emotion.

Now that you've looked at the basic shape of the chart and its elemental balance, you can move on to the placement of the three symbols which, together, most strongly define personality in a natal chart: the Sun, the Moon and the Ascendant.

Simple Analysis of the Moon Position

A good way to begin is to look at the Moon's position by sign, house and aspect. The Moon reveals much about an individual's general orientation, the "day-to-day" personality, even the ``minute-to-minute'' mood or temperament that really defines who an individual is. Even on a basic level, this yields much important information. Consider what can be learned just from the following simple summaries.

ARIES MOON. An Aries Moon reveals an aggressive, but easygoing, almost playful personality, blustery and easily agitated, with strong moods which come and go quickly.

TAURUS MOON. A Taurus Moon reveals an essentially calm and well-grounded personality, slow to agitate, but fierce and passionate once angered or excited, with a powerful stubborn streak and long-lasting moods.

GEMINI MOON. A Gemini Moon reveals an easygoing, social individual for whom curiosity is a powerful drive. This is someone who is easily agitated, but whose moods, feelings, habits and thoughts come and go swiftly, and are always full of change and surprise.

CANCER MOON. A Cancer Moon reveals a sensitive personality, quick to agitate but careful and deliberate in showing its passions, with a defensive, self-protective streak, nurturing inclinations combined with the desire to be nurtured, strong intuition, and colorful, powerful moods.

LEO MOON. A Leo Moon reveals a dramatic personality, quick to agitate and equally quick to voice thoughts and opinions. The urge to take charge is strong, as are the fun-loving, generous qualities of personality and the powerful, influential moods.

VIRGO MOON. A Virgo Moon reveals a highly-strung, precise personality, quick to agitate, with swift reflexes and reactions and much adaptability, combined with a tendency to worry, much attention to detail and powerful sensitivity and moods.

LIBRA MOON. A Libra Moon reveals a refined personality, quick to agitate, but loathe to display any kind of agitation, with a tactful, diplomatic charm, and the desire to promote harmony in all things. Moods, habits and emotions tend to be quite even and steady on the surface, although inwardly they may be extremely sensitive and changeable.

SCORPIO MOON. A Scorpio Moon reveals a powerfully deep personality, slow to agitate, but fierce, once agitated, with passionate feelings, reactions and moods. Expression is very deliberate and self-protective. This lunar placement is emotionally insatiable, craving new and intense experiences of all kinds, but feeling uncomfortable with any loss of emotional control or vulnerability.

SAGITTARIUS MOON. A Sagittarius Moon reveals an adventurous personality, easygoing and quick to agitate, but rarely caught up in deeply emotional quagmires, with a fun-loving, expansive, generous attitude, and generally even-keeled moods.

CAPRICORN MOON. A Capricorn Moon reveals a serious personality, slow to agitate, but passionate once agitated, with a practical outlook and careful, deliberate and generally productive feelings and moods.

AQUARIUS MOON. An Aquarius Moon reveals an aloof personality, quick to agitate, but rarely getting caught up in complicated emotional muddles, with an abrupt and logical approach to emotions, slightly self-centered, yet caring in a detached sort of way. Moods are powerful, though generally short-lived.

PISCES MOON. A Pisces Moon reveals a personality strongly colored by feelings, intuition, mood and emotion, quick to agitate, with a tendency to indulge moods and feelings. It combines a strong emotionality with powerful charm, sensitivity and natural reserve.

These small tidbits of information alone provide plenty of "meat" in chart analysis. Contemplating and discussing how an individual digests life on the instinctual and emotional level, as represented by the natal Moon, goes quite far in providing and understanding of the personality, and gives an astrologer plenty of information to discuss with a client, or think about in his or her own chart.

Bottom Line: The Moon sign alone provides enough energy and symbolism to make an entire natal chart worth looking at. Throw in the lunar house placement and aspects, and the dynamics of just that one symbol—the Moon—are powerful enough to keep you interested in astrology for the rest of your days. In its symbolism is emotional nourishment, the dynamics of your security and feelings, the color and tone of your moods, the roots of your reactions and personality.

Simplicity with the Sun, the Ascendant and Beyond

After considering the Moon, look next at the position of the Sun. The Sun is a symbol of centering. It is the center of you and your ego. While the Moon represents where you are in your everyday self-expression, the Sun symbolizes your larger, more encompassing sense of self and identity. And it represents, not only who you are, but also who you are attempting to become, the sense of identity you're constantly growing into.

After you have looked at the Moon and the Sun, it's time to look at the Ascendant. Some students get rather nervous at this point. The Moon and the Sun are very forthright symbols of personality. Feelings and Ego. The Moon and the Sun are concrete bodies in the sky—the Lights. We can all relate to them. But the Ascendant is not a tangible celestial body. It is an abstract point in space. We haven't grown up according to its visible rhythms, as we have with the Moon and the Sun. The Ascendant is more strictly astrological in nature, much further removed from everyday life. It seems more mystical. The Ascendant can be intimidating.

Whisper: simplicity.

On the most simple, basic, level, the Ascendant represents the window through which you look at the world, and through which the world looks at you. The ascending sign is like the color or tone of the glass which is in the window. Everything you express is colored by that basic Ascendant hue. Everything others see of you is somewhat colored by that same hue.

Remember, the Ascendant is the cusp of the first house. It links the houses with the signs in a chart and is, therefore, a strong symbol, linking spirit with corporeality. The Ascendant is one of the most personalizing symbols in a natal chart, representing the moment in time at which you ``hopped aboard'' the wheel of life through your first breath. It is a symbol of earth meeting sky in your own personal dawn.

To describe the nature of the Ascendant, as well as the interplay between the Ascendant, the Sun and the Moon, let us quote from Beth Huether Koch's book *Equal Houses*:

> The Ascendant does not so much relate to a drive or urge, but more toward a fundamental temperament, an essential way of being...often less conscious, yet more immediate than the identity aspects of either Sun or Moon. Together, the trilogy of Sun, Moon and Ascendant provides human personality with a sense of self that is encompassing (Sun) spontaneous (Moon) and also consistent (Ascendant). You are always growing and changing (Sun) your feelings and moods constantly change (Moon) but through it all, there is a seed-core which is always you. That seed-core's consistent feel is symbolized by the Ascendant.

After analyzing a chart's basic shaping, its elements, the placement of the Sun, Moon and Ascendant, it's time to zero in on some of the specifics. This is the time to take note of the strength of the various planets in the chart. Where is the chart ruler, the planet which rules the rising sign? Are any planets rising or conjoining angles? These planets, and the drives they represent, will be strong forces in the chart, usually almost as important as the Sun, Moon and Ascendant.

By now, you should be developing a pretty good "feel" for the overall "vibration" of the chart, the overall perception of what this individual is like on a very basic level. Notice the words feel and vibration. Don't; just think your way through the chart with your mind. Let yourself feel the chart. Astrology trains to you to cultivate and use your intuition and perceptions as much as your logical mind. Allow the chart to speak to you. Analyze the chart, yes. But gradually cultivate your inclination to feel the chart too. It's in this intuitive and perceptual journey that astrology becomes an art.

At this point you can look at major aspects in the chart, especially stelliums and conjunctions involving the Ascendant, the Sun, the Moon, the chart ruler or the Midheaven, T-square and grand configurations. Look at these in the way we have already described. When confused or in doubt, draw yourself back to basics. What is each individual symbol really about? For example, a T-square is essentially squares linked by an opposition. It is a tense, challenging interplay between planetary energies, probably problematic, but also motivating and productive. A stellium is essentially a series of conjunctions. On a simple level, it is a group of planets working in tandem.

Next, look individually at each of the remaining planetary placements in the chart, considering each by sign, house and aspects.

Recognizing the Themes in A Chart

Generally, by this stage in the interpretation, you will begin to see consistent themes repeating themselves in different places, in different way in the chart. The themes will be saying much the same thing.

For example, perhaps the chart contains a Sun-Uranus trine—independent, rebellious, forward thinking, full of surprises,and so on. Now, you may notice that the chart also has Venus and Mars in Aquarius. Many of the same themes are reemphasized. Now, you see the Moon in the eleventh house. And perhaps some of the other personal planets form aspects with the Sun-Uranus trine and with the Aquarian planets. The same descriptive keywords and the Uranus/Aquarius theme are seen not only in the Sun-Uranus trine, but also throughout the chart. This will obviously be an important theme to emphasize in your analysis. It will color many areas of the individual life and personality.

Sometimes it happens that a chart seems to have a number of conflicting themes, for example a bunch of well-grounded, practical Capricorn/Saturn themes coexisting with a heap of nebulous, emotional Pisces/Neptune themes. Don't fight it. People are complex beings and every one of us is unique. This complexity and uniqueness is reflected in our charts. One personality can be both well-grounded and nebulous in different situations, at different times, and in different areas of temperament, reaction and expression. Not everything about us can be tied up neatly in a nice, tidy astrological package. Part of the process of simplifying chart analysis lies in accepting complexity and loose ends as part of the human condition—and the astrological condition, too!

Wrapping It Up

So, there is a skeletal framework of what to do with a chart once you've drawn it up for yourself or for someone else. Hang in there! Like any other skill or talent, reading a whole chart takes a lot of practice. But, also like anything else, it does become easier with time and experience. Trying to keep things as simple and straightforward as possible helps enormously when you set out to make some sense of the compelling and perpetually significant symbol of the chart.

When you feel like asking, "What do I do now?", the answer might just be: "Enjoy and learn to love the feel of an emerging chart." Take your time and take a leap of faith, allowing your intuition and perceptual mind to tell you as much about the chart as your intellect does. Practice the art of astrology and be open to its experience. And always remember the mantra: simplicity!

Practice Exercises

Using the birth data below, calculate the four practice charts. The completed Worksheets and computer-calculated charts are found on the following pages.

Richard Roe
November 5, 1980
2:15 p.m. PST
Los Angeles, California; 34N03′08″, 118W14′34″

Mary Moe
June 10, 1965
10:25 p.m. MDT
Denver, Colorado; 39N44′21″, 104W59′03″

Wong Doe
October 1, 1986
1:35 a.m. AWST (-8)
Beijing, China; 39N55′, 116E25′

Kanga Roe
April 6, 1975
11:32 p.m. AEST (-10)
Sydney, NSW, Australia; 33S52′, 151E13′

NATAL CHART WORKSHEET 1
Birth Data

Name: *RICHARD ROE*   Source of data: *SUBJECT*

Date of birth: *NOVEMBER 5, 1980*

Time of birth (incl. time zone): *2:15 P.M. PST*

Place of birth: *LOS ANGELES, CALIFORNIA*

Latitude: *34 N03'08*   Longitude: *118W14'34*   Time zone correction: *7:52:58*
                                                     (long x 4 mins.)

TLT calculation

Clock birth time: *14: 15: 00*

- 1 hour if DT/WT:

Local standard birth time: *14: 15: 00*

+/- mins. of time zone corr:: *+ 07: 02*

TLT=   *14: 22: 02*

GMT birth time calculation

Method 1		*Method 2*	
TLT:	*14:22:02*	Local standard time:	*14:15:00*
Time zone corr:	*07: 52: 58*	Interval from GMT:	*08: 00: 00*
(+ if W of Greenwich - if E of Greenwich)			
GMT birth time =	*22: 15: 00*		*22: 15: 00*

RICHARD ROE   **NATAL CHART WORKSHEET 2**
Sidereal time calculation

Sid. time at Greenwich
midnight previous to TLT: *02 : 57 : 30*

+/- longitude corr: *+ 01 : 19*   long corr in secs = 2/3 long of place of birth
                                             + W of Greenwich, - if E

Corrected sid. time: *02 : 58 : 49*

+ interval   *14 : 22 : 02*
TLT-previous midnight:

+ acceleration of interval::   *02 : 24*   = 10 secs/hour, 1 sec/6 mins of interval

Calculated sid. time: *17 : 23 : 15*

Note: add 12 hours for Southern Hemisphere birth

Closest sid. times in table of houses: earlier: *17:20:00*   later: *17:24:00*

Sidereal time factor calculation

Calculated sid. time: *17 : 23 : 15*

- closest earlier sid. time: *17 : 20 : 00*

Difference in seconds: *195 =*   *03 : 15*

STF = (difference/240) =   *0.8125*

Latitude factor calculation

Minutes of latitude: *03' 08*

LF = (minutes of latitude/60) =   *0.05222*

RICHARD ROE   **NATAL CHART WORKSHEET 3**

House cusps: Sidereal time adjustment

Closest sid times: earlier: 17:20   later: 17:24
Closest latitudes: lower: 34   higher: 35
STF = 0.8125

Use lower latitude:

	10(MC)	11	12	1(Asc)	2	3
cusp later sid. time:	21 ✗ 44	11 ♑ 19	10 ♒ 17	16 ♓ 13	27 ♈ 53	27 ♉ 55
cusp earlier sid. time:	20 ✗ 49	13 ♑ 22	9 ♒ 08	14 ♓ 43	26 ♈ 36	26 ♉ 54
Distance in minutes:	55	57	69	90	77	61
Distance x STF	(0.8125)					
Sid. time correction:	44.6875	46.3125	56.0625	73.125	62.5625	49.5625
+ mins. of cusp earlier sid. time:	49	22	08	43	36	54
Cusp adjusted for sid. time:	21✗33.6875	14♑08.3125	10♒04.0625	15♓56.125	27♈38.5625	27♉43.5625

Final 10th house cusp = 21 ✗ 34

RICHARD ROE   **NATAL CHART WORKSHEET 4**

House cusps: Latitude adjustment

Closest sid. times: earlier: 17:20   later: 17:24
Closest latitudes: lower: 34   higher: 35
LF = 0.05222

Use earlier sid. time:

	11	12	1(Asc)	2	3
cusp at higher lat:	13♑09	8♒46	14✶28	26♈50	27♉05
cusp at lower lat:	13♑22	9♒08	14✶43	26♈36	26♉54
Distance in mins:	13	22	15	14	11
Distance x LF	(0.05222)				
LF correction:	0.67886	1.14884	0.7833	0.73108	0.57442
Cusp adjusted for sid. time: (from p.3)	14♑08.3125	10♒04.625	15✶56.125	27♈38.5625	27♉43.5625
+/- latitude correction: (If higher is higher, add)	−0.67886	−1.14884	−0.7833	+0.73108	+0.57442

Corrected cusps: 14♑07.6   10♒02.91   15✶55.34   27♈39.29   27♉44.1
Final cusps (rounded up or down):
Note: reverse for Southern Hemisphere birth
10 21♐34 11 14♑08 12 10♒03 1 15✶55 2 27♈39 3 27♉44

4 21♊34 5 14♋08 6 10♌03 7 15♍55 8 27♎39 9 27♏44

Richard Roe   **NATAL CHART WORKSHEET 5**

Planetary positions: Luminaries

GMT birth time: 22:15:00   Decimalized: 22.25
GMT birth date: November 5, 1980

	☉	☽
Position midnight day after GMT birth date:	13 ♏ 43 52	23 ♎ 24 53
Position midnight GMT birth date:	12 43 45	11 34 32
Distance in 24 hours:	1 00 07	11 50 21
	(60.11666)	(11.83916)
(Distance/24) x interval birth time - previous midnight:	(60.11666/24) x 22.25	(÷ 24 x 22.25)
Actual travel:	00 : 55 : 44	10 : 58 : 33
Starting position (midnight birth date):	12 ♏ 43 45	11 ♎ 34 32
+ actual travel:	55 44	10 58 33
Position:	13 ♏ 39 29	22 ♎ 33 05

49

Richard Roe   **NATAL CHART WORKSHEET 6**

Planetary positions: Inner planets

GMT birth time: 22:15:00 Decimalized: 22.25
GMT birth date: November 5, 1980

	☿	♀	♂
Position midnight day after GMT birth date:	7 ♏ 53.2 ℞	7 ♎ 55.0	17 ♐ 57.8
Position midnight GMT birth date:	9 04.5 ℞	6 42.3	17 13.4
Distance in 24 hours:	1 11.3	1 12.7	44.4
	(71.3)	(72.7)	
(Distance/24) x interval birth time - previous midnight:	(÷ 24 × 22.25)	(÷ 24 × 22.25)	(÷ 24 × 22.25)
Actual travel:	66.1	67.4	41.1
	(1:06.1)	(1:07.4)	
Starting position (midnight birth date):	9 ♏ 04.5 ℞	6 ♎ 42.3	17 ♐ 13.4
+ actual travel (- if retrograde)	− 1 06.1	+ 1 07.4	+ 41.1
Position:	7 ♏ 58.4 ℞	7 ♎ 49.7	17 ♐ 54.5

RICHARD ROE   **NATAL CHART WORKSHEET 7**

Planetary positions: ♃ ♄ ♅

GMT birth time: 22:15:00 Decimalized: 22.25
GMT birth date: NOVEMBER 5, 1980

	♃	♄	♅
Position midnight day after GMT birth date:	1 ♎ 50.0	5 ♎ 23.7	25 ♏ 6.9
Position midnight GMT birth date:	1 38.8	5 17.3	25 3.2
Distance in 24 hours:	11.2	6.4	3.7
(Distance/24) x interval birth time - previous midnight:	(÷ 24 × 22.25)		
Actual travel:	10.4	5.9	3.4
Starting position (midnight birth date):	1 ♎ 38.8	5 ♎ 17.3	25 ♏ 3.2
+ actual travel (- if retrograde)	+ 10.4	+ 5.9	+ 3.4
Position:	1 ♎ 49.2	5 ♎ 23.2	25 ♏ 6.6

NATAL CHART WORKSHEET 8

Plantary positions: ♆ ♀ ☊

GMT birth time: 22:15:00 Decimalized: 22.25
GMT birth date: NOVEMBER 5, 1980

	♆	♀	☊
Position midnight day after GMT birth date:	21 ♐ 01.6	22 ♎ 33.7	15 ♌ 59.5 ℞
Position midnight GMT birth date:	20 59.7	22 31.5	16 ♌ 11.5 ℞
Distance in 24 hours:	1.9	2.2	12.0
(Distance/24) x interval birth time - previous midnight:	(÷ 24 x 22.25)		
Actual travel:	1.7	2.0	11.1
Starting position (midnight birth date):	20 ♐ 59.7	22 ♎ 31.5	16 ♌ 11.5 ℞
+ actual travel: (- if retrograde)	+ 1.7	+ 2.0	- 11.1
Position:	21 ♐ 01.4	22 ♎ 33.5	16 ♌ 0.4 ℞

Position of ☊ = 16 ♒ 0.4 ℞

Richard Roe   **NATAL CHART WORKSHEET 9**
Chiron, Part of Fortune, Part of Spirit

⚷

Position 1st day of month after birth month::   14 ♉ 42.6 ♃

Position 1st day birth month: 16   10.9 ♃

Distance in month: 1   28.3   (88.3)

(Distance/number of days in month) *x*
number of birth date: (÷ 30 × 5)

Actual travel: 14.7

Starting position (1st day of birth month):   16 ♉ 10.9 ♃

+ actual travel: − 14.7
(- *if retrograde*)

Position: 15 ♉ 56.2 ♃

⊗   ☿
(Diurnal charts - reverse for nocturnal)

Ascendant:	12	15	55		Ascendant:	12	15	55
+ Moon	07	22	33		+ Sun	08	13	39
	20	08	28			20	29	34
- Sun	08	13	39		- Moon	07	22	33
Position:	11	24	49			13	07	01
					(01)			

⊗ = 24 ♒ 49   ☿ = 7 ♈ 01

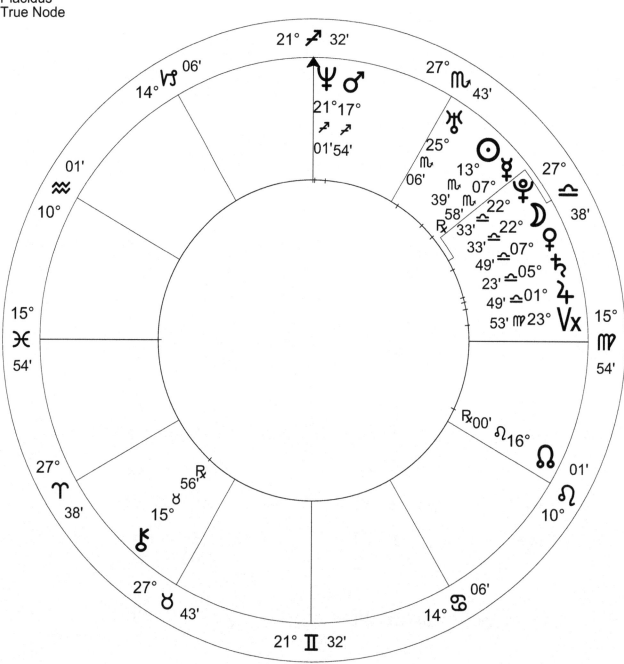

NATAL CHART WORKSHEET 1
Birth Data

Name: MARY MOE   Source of data: SUBJECT

Date of birth: JUNE 10, 1965

Time of birth (incl. time zone): 10:25 P.M. MDT

Place of birth: DENVER, COLORADO

Latitude: 39 N 44' 21   Longitude: 104 W 59' 03   Time zone correction: 6:59:56
(long x 4 mins.)

TLT calculation

Clock birth time: 22:25:00

- 1 hour if DT/WT: 01:00:00

Local standard birth time: 21:25:00

+/- mins. of time zone corr: 00:00:04

TLT=   21:25:04

GMT birth time calculation

Method 1		*Method 2*	
TLT:	21:25:04	Local standard time:	21:25:00
Time zone corr:	6:59:56	Interval from GMT:	07:00:00

(+ if W of Greenwich
- if E of Greenwich)

GMT birth time =   04:25:00   04:25:00
                     JUNE 11, 1965   JUNE 11, 1965

MARY MOE   **NATAL CHART WORKSHEET 2**
Sidereal time calculation

Sid. time at Greenwich
midnight previous to TLT: 17 : 12 : 33

+/- longitude corr: + 01 : 10   long corr in secs = 2/3 long of place of birth
_____   + W of Greenwich, - if E

Corrected sid. time: 17 : 13 : 43

+ interval
TLT-previous midnight: 21 : 25 : 04

+ acceleration of interval: 03 : 34   = 10 secs/hour, 1 sec/6 mins of interval
_____

Calculated sid. time: 38 : 42 : 21
(14)
Note: add 12 hours for Southern Hemisphere birth

Closest sid. times in table of houses: earlier: 14 : 40 : 00 later: 14 : 44 : 00

Sidereal time factor calculation

Calculated sid. time: 14 : 42 : 21

- closest earlier sid. time: 14 : 40 : 00
_____

Difference in seconds: |4| =   02 : 21

STF = (difference/240) =   0.5875

Latitude factor calculation

Minutes of latitude: 44'21

LF = (minutes of latitude/60) =   0.73916

56

MARY MOE   *NATAL CHART WORKSHEET 3*

House cusps: Sidereal time adjustment

Closest sid times: earlier: 14:40   later: 14:44
Closest latitudes: lower: 39   higher: 40
STF = 0.5875

Use lower latitude:

	10(MC)	11	12	1(Asc)	2	3
cusp later sid. time:	13 ♏ 27	6 ♐ 40	27 ♐ 32	20 ♑ 20	3 ♓ 28	13 ♈ 32
cusp earlier sid. time:	12 ♏ 27	5 ♐ 46	26 ♐ 38	19 ♑ 15	2 ♓ 08	12 ♈ 18
Distance in minutes:	60	54	54	65	80	74
Distance x STF (0.5875)						
Sid. time correction:	35.25	31.725	31.725	38.1875	47	43.475
+ mins. of cusp earlier sid. time:	27	46	38	15	08	18
Cusp adjusted for sid. time:	13 ♏ 2.25	6 ♐ 17.725	27 ♐ 9.725	19 ♑ 53.1875	2 ♓ 55	13 ♈ 01.475

Final 10th house cusp = 13 ♏ 02

57

Mary Moe   **NATAL CHART WORKSHEET 4**

House cusps: Latitude adjustment

Closest sid. times: earlier: *14:40*   later: *14:44*
Closest latitudes: lower: *39*   higher: *40*
LF = *0.73916*

Use earlier sid. time:

	11	12	1(Asc)	2	3
cusp at higher lat:	5♐34	26♐09	18♑28	1♓51	12♈22
cusp at lower lat:	5♐46	26♐38	19♑15	2♓08	12♈18
Distance in mins:	12	29	47	17	4
Distance x LF	(0.73916)				
LF correction:	8.86992	21.4356A	34.74052	12.56572	2.9566A
Cusp adjusted for sid. time: (from p.3)	6♐17.725	27♐9.725	18♑53.1875	2♓55	13♈1.475
+/- latitude correction: (If higher is higher, add)	−8.86992	−21.4356A	−34.74052	−12.56572	+2.9566A
Corrected cusps:	6♐08.85	26♐48.2	18♑18.44	2♓42.43	13♈4.43

Final cusps (rounded up or down):
Note: reverse for Southern Hemisphere birth

10 *13♏02* 11 *6♐09* 12 *26♐48* 1 *18♑18* 2 *2♓42* 3 *13♈04*

4 *13♉02* 5 *6♊09* 6 *26♊48* 7 *18♋18* 8 *2♍42* 9 *13♎04*

MARY MOE   **NATAL CHART WORKSHEET 5**

Planetary positions: Luminaries

GMT birth time: *04:25:00* Decimalized: *4.41666*
GMT birth date: *JUNE 11, 1965*

	☉	☽
Position midnight day after GMT birth date:	20 Ⅱ 48 54	27 ♏ 20 13
Position midnight GMT birth date:	19 51 35	14 50 00
Distance in 24 hours:	57 19	12 30 13
(Distance/24) *x* interval birth time - previous midnight:	(57.31666) (÷ 24 × 4.41666)	(12.50361)
Actual travel:	10 33	2 18 04
Starting position (midnight birth date):	19 Ⅱ 51 35	14 ♏ 50 00
+ actual travel:	10 33	2 18 04
Position:	20 Ⅱ 02 08	17 ♏ 08 04

59

MARY MOE   **NATAL CHART WORKSHEET 6**

Planetary positions: Inner planets

GMT birth time: *04:25:00* Decimalized: *4.41666*

GMT birth date: *JUNE 11, 1965*

	☿	♀	♂
Position midnight day after GMT birth date:	21 ♊ 04.4	6 ♋ 54.2	22 ♍ 02.9
Position midnight GMT birth date:	18 52.3	5 40.8	21 37.2
Distance in 24 hours:	2 12.1	1 13.4	25.7
(Distance/24) x interval birth time - previous midnight:	(132.1)	(73.4)	
	(÷ 24 x 4.41666)		
Actual travel:	24.3	13.5	4.7
Starting position (midnight birth date):	18 ♊ 52.3	5 ♋ 40.8	21 ♍ 37.2
+ actual travel (- if retrograde)	+ 24.3	+ 13.5	+ 4.7
Position:	19 ♊ 16.6	5 ♋ 54.3	21 ♍ 41.9

MARY MOE **NATAL CHART WORKSHEET 7**

Planetary positions: ♃ ♄ ♅

GMT birth time: 04:25:00 Decimalized: 4.41666
GMT birth date: JUNE 11, 1965

	♃	♄	♅
Position midnight day after GMT birth date:	11 ♊ 37.0	17 ♓ 00.2	10 ♍ 57.5
Position midnight GMT birth date:	11 23.1	16 58.5	10 56.3
Distance in 24 hours:	13.9	1.7	1.2
(Distance/24) x interval birth time - previous midnight:	(÷ 24 × 4.41666)		
Actual travel:	2.5	0.3	0.2
Starting position (midnight birth date):	11 ♊ 23.1	16 ♓ 58.5	10 ♍ 56.3
+ actual travel (- *if retrograde*)	+ 2.5	+ 0.3	+ 0.2
Position:	11 ♊ 25.6	16 ♓ 58.8	10 ♍ 56.5

MARY MOE **NATAL CHART WORKSHEET 8**

Plantary positions: ♆ ♀ ☊

GMT birth time: *04:25:00* Decimalized: *4.41666*
GMT birth date: *JUNE 11, 1965*

	♆	♀	☊
Position midnight day after GMT birth date:	*17 ♏ 47.5 ℞*	*13 ♍ 45.7*	*13 ♊ 50.8*
Position midnight GMT birth date:	*17 48.8 ℞*	*13 45.2*	*13 50.3*
Distance in 24 hours:	*1.3*	*0.5*	*0.5*
(Distance/24) x interval birth time - previous midnight:	*(÷24 × 4.41666)*		
Actual travel:	*0.2*	*0.1*	*0.1*
Starting position (midnight birth date):	*17 ♏ 48.8 ℞*	*13 ♍ 45.2*	*13 ♊ 50.3*
+ actual travel: (- if retrograde)	*– 0.2*	*+ 0.1*	*+ 0.1*
Position:	*17 ♏ 48.6 ℞*	*13 ♍ 45.3*	*13 ♊ 50.4*

Position of ☋ = *13 ♐ 50.4*

MARY MOE   **NATAL CHART WORKSHEET 9**
           Chiron, Part of Fortune, Part of Spirit

                              ⚷

Position 1st day of month after birth month::   22 ✳ 32.9 ℞

Position 1st day birth month: 22 ✳ 17.7

Distance in month: 15.2

(Distance/number of days in month) *x*
number of birth date: (÷ 30 × 11)

Actual travel: 5.0

Starting position (1st day of birth month):   22 ✳ 17.7

+ actual travel: +   5.0
(– *if retrograde*)

Position: 22 ✳ 22.7 (APPROXIMATE)

          ⊕   ⊖
              (Diurnal charts – reverse for nocturnal)

Ascendant: 10   19   18   Ascendant: 10   19   18

+ Moon   08   17   09   + Sun   03   20   02
              _____   _____
                19   06   27   14   09   20

– Sun   03   20   02   – Moon   08   17   09

Position: 15   16   25   05   22   11
              (03)

        ⊕:   16 ♊ 25   ⊖ = 22 ♌ 11

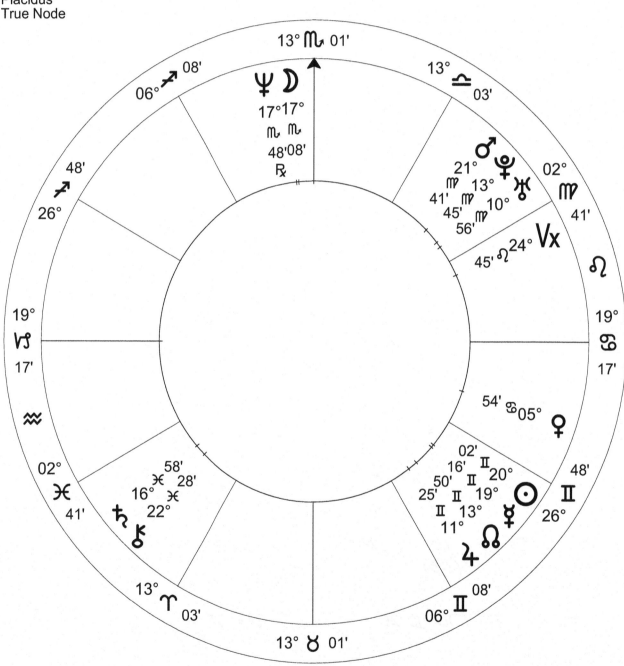

Mary Moe
Natal Chart
Jun 10 1965, Thu
10:25 pm MDT +6:00
Denver, CO
39°N44'21" 104°W59'03"
Geocentric
Tropical
Placidus
True Node

NATAL CHART WORKSHEET 1
Birth Data

Name: WONG DOE   Source of data: SUBJECT

Date of birth: OCTOBER 1, 1986

Time of birth (incl. time zone): 1:35 A.M. [GMT -8]

Place of birth: PRC - BEIJING

Latitude: 39 N 55   Longitude: 116 E 25   Time zone correction: − 7:45:40
(long x 4 mins.)

TLT calculation

Clock birth time: 01:35:00

- 1 hour if DT/WT: −

Local standard birth time: 01:35:00

+/- mins. of time zone corr::   − 14:20

TLT=   01:20:40

GMT birth time calculation

Method 1		*Method 2*	
TLT:	01:20:40	Local standard time:	01:35:00
Time zone corr:	−07:45:40	Interval from GMT:	−08:00:00

(+ if W of Greenwich
- if E of Greenwich)

GMT birth time =   17:35:00   17:35:00
                    SEPTEMBER 30, 1986   SEPTEMBER 30, 1986

WONG DOE

NATAL CHART WORKSHEET 2
Sidereal time calculation

Sid. time at Greenwich
midnight previous to TLT: 00 : 37 : 44

+/- longitude corr: − 01 : 17   long corr in secs = 2/3 long of place of birth
                                                + W of Greenwich, - if E
_____

Corrected sid. time: 00 : 36 : 27

+ interval
TLT-previous midnight: 01 : 20 : 40

+ acceleration of interval::   13   = 10 secs/hour, 1 sec/6 mins of interval
_____

Calculated sid. time: 01 : 57 : 20

Note: add 12 hours for Southern Hemisphere birth

Closest sid. times in table of houses: earlier: 01 : 56   later: 02 : 00

Sidereal time factor calculation

Calculated sid. time: 01 : 57 : 20

- closest earlier sid. time: 01 : 56 : 00
_____

Difference in seconds: 80 =   1 : 20

STF = (difference/240) =   0.33333

Latitude factor calculation

Minutes of latitude: 55

LF = (minutes of latitude/60) =   0.91666

WONG DOE   *NATAL CHART WORKSHEET 3*

House cusps: Sidereal time adjustment

Closest sid times: earlier: 01:56   later: 02:00
Closest latitudes: lower: 39   higher: 40
STF = 0.33333

Use lower latitude:

	10(MC)	11	12	1(Asc)	2	3
cusp later sid. time:	28 ♉ 11	8 ♊ 01	12 ♋ 15	12 ♌ 03	3 ♍ 39	0 ♎ 00
cusp earlier sid. time:	18 ♉ 08	7 ♊ 01	11 ♋ 23	11 ♌ 15	2 ♍ 47	29 ♍ 01
Distance in minutes:	63	60	52	48	52	59
Distance x STF	(0.33333)					
Sid. time correction:	21	20	17.33316	16	17.33316	19.66647
+ mins. of cusp earlier sid. time:	08	01	23	15	47	01
Cusp adjusted for sid. time:	18 ♉ 29	7 ♊ 21	11 ♋ 40.33316	11 ♌ 31	3 ♍ 4.33316	29 ♍ 20.666

Final 10th house cusp =   18 ♉ 29

WONG DOE

NATAL CHART WORKSHEET 4

House cusps: Latitude adjustment

Closest sid. times: earlier: 01:56   later: 02:00
Closest latitudes: lower: 39   higher: 40
LF = 0.91666

Use earlier sid. time:

	11	12	1(Asc)	2	3
cusp at higher lat:	7 ♊ 15	11 ♋ 49	11 ♌ 41	2 ♍ 58	29 ♍ 02
cusp at lower lat:	7 ♊ 01	11 ♋ 23	11 ♌ 15	2 ♍ 47	29 ♍ 01
Distance in mins:	14	26	26	11	1
Distance x LF	(0.91666)				
LF correction:	12.83324	23.83316	23.83316	10.08326	0.91666
Cusp adjusted for sid. time: (from p.3)	7 ♊ 21	11 ♋ 40.33316	11 ♌ 31	3 ♍ 4.33316	29 ♍ 20.66647
+/- latitude correction: (If higher is higher, add)	+12.83324	+23.83316	+23.83316	+10.08326	+0.91666

Corrected cusps: 7 ♊ 32.8   12 ♋ 4.16   11 ♌ 54.8   3 ♍ 14.41   29 ♍ 21.5
Final cusps (rounded up or down):
Note: reverse for Southern Hemisphere birth

10 1 ♉ 29   11 7 ♊ 33   12 12 ♋ 04   1 11 ♌ 55   2 3 ♍ 14   3 29 ♍ 21

4 1 ♏ 29   5 7 ♐ 33   6 12 ♑ 04   7 11 ♒ 55   8 3 ♓ 14   9 29 ♓ 21

WONG DOE   **NATAL CHART WORKSHEET 5**

Planetary positions: Luminaries

GMT birth time: 17:35   Decimalized: 17.58333
GMT birth date: SEPTEMBER 30, 1986

	☉	☽
Position midnight day after GMT birth date:	7 ♎ 31 19	2 ♍ 43 28
Position midnight GMT birth date:	6 32 20	19 ♌ 53 08
Distance in 24 hours:	58 59 (58.98333)	12 50 20 (12.83888)
(Distance/24) x interval birth time - previous midnight:	(÷ 24 × 17.58333)	
Actual travel:	43 13	9 24 23
Starting position (midnight birth date):	6 ♎ 32 20	19 ♌ 53 08
+ actual travel:	43 13	9 24 23
Position:	7 ♎ 15 33	29 ♌ 17 31

WONG DOE   **NATAL CHART WORKSHEET 6**

Planetary positions: Inner planets

GMT birth time: 17:35   Decimalized: 17.58333
GMT birth date: SEPTEMBER 30, 1986

	☿	♀	♂
Position midnight day after GMT birth date:	25 ♎ 35.6	16 ♏ 36.0	25 ♑ 46.4
Position midnight GMT birth date:	24 6.0	16 6.4	25 16.4
Distance in 24 hours:	1 29.6	29.6	30.0
(Distance/24) x interval birth time - previous midnight:	(89.6) (÷ 24 × 17.58333)		
Actual travel:	65.6 (1: 05.6)	21.6	22.0
Starting position (midnight birth date):	24 ♎ 6.0	16 ♏ 6.4	25 ♑ 16.4
+ actual travel (- if retrograde)	+ 1 5.6	+ 21.6	+ 22.0
Position:	25 ♎ 11.6	16 ♏ 28	25 ♑ 38.4

70

NATAL CHART WORKSHEET 7

WONG DOE   *Planetary positions:* ♃ ♄ ♅

GMT birth time: 17:35   Decimalized: 17.58333
GMT birth date: SEPTEMBER 30, 1986

	♃	♄	♅
Position midnight day after GMT birth date:	15✶19.5 ℞	5✗ 22.8	18✗51.1
Position midnight GMT birth date:	15 26.4 ℞	5 18.0	18 49.4
Distance in 24 hours:	6.9	4.8	1.7
(Distance/24) x interval birth time - previous midnight:	(÷ 24 × 17.58333)		
Actual travel:	5.0	3.5	1.2
Starting position (midnight birth date):	15✶26.4 ℞	5✗ 18.0	18✗49.4
+ actual travel (- if retrograde)	− 5.0	+ 3.5	+ 1.2
Position:	15✶21.4 ℞	5✗ 21.5	18✗ 50.6

JOHN DOE   **NATAL CHART WORKSHEET 8**

Planetary positions: Ψ $\female$ $\mathcal{U}$

GMT birth time: 17:35   Decimalized: 17.58333
GMT birth date: SEPTEMBER 30, 1986

	Ψ	$\female$	$\mathcal{U}$
Position midnight day after GMT birth date:	3 ♑ 6.7	6 ♏ 7.0	20 ♈ 55.2 ℞
Position midnight GMT birth date:	3 6.1	6 4.8	20 57.2 ℞
Distance in 24 hours:	0.6	2.2	2.0
(Distance/24) x interval birth time - previous midnight:	(÷ 24 × 17.58333)		
Actual travel:	0.4	1.6	1.4
Starting position (midnight birth date):	3 ♑ 6.1	6 ♏ 4.8	20 ♈ 57.2 ℞
+ actual travel: (- if retrograde)	+ 0.4	+ 1.6	- 1.4
Position:	3 ♑ 6.5	6 ♏ 6.4	20 ♈ 55.8 ℞

Position of $\mathcal{U}$ = 20 ♎ 56 ℞

NATAL CHART WORKSHEET 9
Chiron, Part of Fortune, Part of Spirit

⚷

Position 1st day of month after birth month::

Position 1st day birth month:

Distance in month: NEGLIGIBLE = POSITION ON

(Distance/number of days in month) *x*   OCTOBER 1, 1986
number of birth date:

Actual travel:

Starting position (1st day of birth month):

+ actual travel:
(- if retrograde)

Position: 21 ♊ 22 ℞

↓ ⊕   ☿ ⊗

(Diurnal charts - reverse for <u>nocturnal</u>)

Ascendant:	05 11 54	Ascendant:	05 11 54
+ Moon	05 29 15	+ Sun	07 07 15
	11 11 09		12 19 09
- Sun	07 07 15	- Moon	05 29 15
Position:	04 03 54		06 19 54
	↑= 3 ♋ 54		⊗= 19 ♍ 54

73

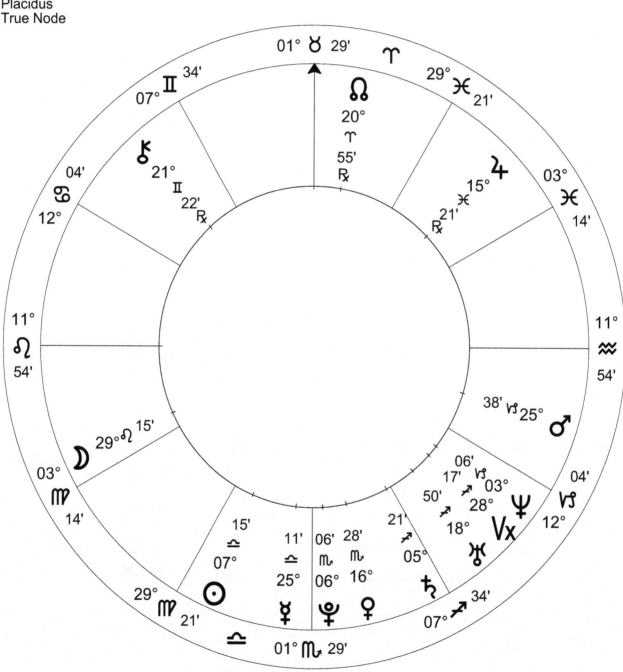

Wong Doe
Natal Chart
Oct 1 1986, Wed
1:35 am AWST −8:00
Beijing, China
39°N55' 116°E25'
Geocentric
Tropical
Placidus
True Node

NATAL CHART WORKSHEET 1
Birth Data

Name: KANGA ROE   Source of data: SUBJECT

Date of birth: APRIL 6, 1975

Time of birth (incl. time zone): 11:32 P.M. [GMT -10] AEST

Place of birth: SYDNEY, NSW, AUSTRALIA

Latitude: 33 S 52   Longitude: 151 E 13   Time zone correction: -10:04:52
                                              (long x 4 mins.)

TLT calculation

Clock birth time: 23:32:00

- 1 hour if DT/WT: —

Local standard birth time: 23:32:00

+/- mins. of time zone corr: + 04:52

TLT=   23:36:52

GMT birth time calculation

Method 1		*Method 2*	
TLT:	23:36:52	Local standard time:	23:32:00
Time zone corr:	-10:04:52	Interval from GMT:	-10:00:00
(+ if W of Greenwich - if E of Greenwich)			
GMT birth time =	13:32:00		13:32:00

KANGA ROE   **NATAL CHART WORKSHEET 2**
Sidereal time calculation

Sid. time at Greenwich
midnight previous to TLT: 12:54:39

+/- longitude corr: $-$ 01:41   long corr in secs = 2/3 long of place of birth
                                           + W of Greenwich, - if E

Corrected sid. time: 12:52:58

+ interval
TLT-previous midnight: 23:36:52

+ acceleration of interval::   03:56   = 10 secs/hour, 1 sec/6 mins of interval

Calculated sid. time: 36:33:46
                           (12)
✓*Note: add 12 hours for Southern Hemisphere birth* = 24(00):33:46

Closest sid. times in table of houses: earlier: 00:32   later: 00:36

Sidereal time factor calculation

Calculated sid. time: 00:33:46

- closest earlier sid. time: 00:32:00

Difference in seconds: 106 =   01:46

STF = (difference/240) =   0.44166

Latitude factor calculation

Minutes of latitude: 52

LF = (minutes of latitude/60) =   0.86666

KANGA ROE   **NATAL CHART WORKSHEET 3**

House cusps: Sidereal time adjustment

Closest sid times: earlier: **00:32**   later: **00:36**
Closest latitudes: lower: **33**   higher: **34**
STF = **0.44166**

Use lower latitude:

	10(MC)	11	12	1(Asc)	2	3
cusp later sid. time:	9 ♈ 48	15 ♉ 08	20 ♊ 33	22 ♋ 09	13 ♌ 59	9 ♍ 11
cusp earlier sid. time:	8 ♈ 43	14 ♉ 03	19 ♊ 36	21 ♋ 18	13 ♌ 07	8 ♍ 12
Distance in minutes:	65	65	57	51	52	59
Distance x STF	(0.44166)					
Sid. time correction:	28.7079	28.7079	25.17462	22.52466	22.96632	26.05794
+ mins. of cusp earlier sid. time:	43	03	36	18	07	12
Cusp adjusted for sid. time:	9 ♈ 11.7079	14 ♉ 31.7079	20 ♊ 1.17462	21 ♋ 40.52466	13 ♌ 29.96632	8 ♍ 38.05794

Final 10th house cusp = **9 ♈ 12**

KANGA ROE   **NATAL CHART WORKSHEET 4**

House cusps: Latitude adjustment

Closest sid. times: earlier: 00:32   later: 00:36
Closest latitudes: lower: 33   higher: 34
LF = 0.86666

Use earlier sid. time:

	11	12	1(Asc)	2	3
cusp at higher lat:	14♉12	20♊01	21♋48	13♌22	8♍17
cusp at lower lat:	14♉03	19♊36	21♋18	13♌07	8♍12
Distance in mins:	9	25	30	15	5
Distance x LF (0.86666)					
LF correction:	7.79994	21.6666	26	13	4.33333

Cusp adjusted
for sid. time: 14♉31.7079   20♊1.17462   21♋40.52466   13♌29.96632   8♍38.05194
(from p.3)

+/- latitude
correction: + 7.79994   +21.6661♉   +26   +13   +4.33333
(If higher is
higher, add)

Corrected cusps: 14♉39.5   20♊22.84   22♋06.5   13♌42.9   8♍42.39
Final cusps (rounded up or down):
✓ *Note: reverse for Southern Hemisphere birth*

10 9♎12   11 14♏39   12 20♐23   1 22♑06   2 13♒43   3 8♓42

4 9♈12   5 14♉39   6 20♊23   7 22♋06   8 13♌43   9 8♍42

KANGA ROE   **NATAL CHART WORKSHEET 5**

Planetary positions: Luminaries

GMT birth time: *13:32*   Decimalized: *13.53333*
GMT birth date: *APRIL 6, 1975*

	☉	☽
Position midnight day after GMT birth date:	16 ♈ 33 28	24 ♒ 55 35
Position midnight GMT birth date:	15 34 24	13 03 51
Distance in 24 hours:	59 04	11 51 44
	(59.06666)	(11.86222)
(Distance/24) x interval birth time - previous midnight:	(÷ 24 x 13.53333)	
Actual travel:	33 18	6 41 20
Starting position (midnight birth date):	15 ♈ 34 24	13 ♒ 03 51
+ actual travel:	33 18	6 41 20
Position:	16 ♈ 07 42	19 ♒ 45 11

KANGA ROE   NATAL CHART WORKSHEET 6

Planetary positions: Inner planets

GMT birth time: 13:32 Decimalized: 13.53333
GMT birth date: APRIL 6, 1975

	☿	♀	♂
Position midnight day after GMT birth date:	4 ♈ 32.0	21 ♉ 46.2	26 ♒ 20.5
Position midnight GMT birth date:	2 41.3	20 34.6	25 34.8
Distance in 24 hours:	1 50.7	1 11.6	45.7
(Distance/24) x interval birth time - previous midnight:	(110.7) (÷24 x 13.53333)	(71.6)	
Actual travel:	62.4 (1:02.4)	40.3	25.7
Starting position (midnight birth date):	2 ♈ 41.3	20 ♉ 34.6	25 ♒ 34.8
+ actual travel (- if retrograde)	+ 1 02.4	+ 40.3	+ 25.7
Position:	3 ♈ 43.7	21 ♉ 14.9	26 ♒ 00.5

80

KANGA ROE   **NATAL CHART WORKSHEET 7**

Planetary positions: ♃ ♄ ♅

GMT birth time: *13:32* Decimalized: *13.53333*
GMT birth date: *APRIL 6, 1975*

	♃	♄	♅
Position midnight day after GMT birth date:	4 ♈ 39.6	12 ♋ 27.5	1 ♏ 2.7 ℞
Position midnight GMT birth date:	4 25.2	12 25.0	1 5.2 ℞
Distance in 24 hours:	14.4	2.5	2.5
(Distance/24) x interval birth time - previous midnight:	(÷ 24 x 13.53333)		
Actual travel:	8.1	1.4	1.4
Starting position (midnight birth date):	4 ♈ 25.2	12 ♋ 25.0	1 ♏ 5.2 ℞
+ actual travel (- if retrograde)	+ 8.1	+ 1.4	- 1.4
Position:	4 ♈ 33.3	12 ♋ 26.4	1 ♏ 3.8 ℞

KANGA ROE   **NATAL CHART WORKSHEET 8**

Plantary positions: ♆ ♀ ☋

GMT birth time: *13:32*   Decimalized: *13.53333*
GMT birth date:
   APRIL 6, 1975

	♆	♀	☋
Position midnight day after GMT birth date:	11 ♐ 38.8 ℞	7 ♎ 39.2 ℞	2 ♐ 1.6 ℞
Position midnight GMT birth date:	11 39.5 ℞	7 40.8 ℞	2 7.2 ℞
Distance in 24 hours:	0.7	1.6	5.6
(Distance/24) x interval birth time - previous midnight:	(÷ 24 x 13.53333)		
Actual travel:	0.4	0.9	3.1
Starting position (midnight birth date):	11 ♐ 39.5 ℞	7 ♎ 40.8 ℞	2 ♐ 7.2 ℞
+ actual travel: (- if retrograde)	− 0.4	− 0.9	− 3.1
Position:	11 ♐ 39.1 ℞	7 ♎ 39.9 ℞	2 ♐ 4.1 ℞

Position of ☋ = *2 ♊ 4.1 ℞*

KANGA ROE   **NATAL CHART WORKSHEET 9**
Chiron, Part of Fortune, Part of Spirit

⚷

Position 1st day of month after birth month: 24 ♈ 56.5

Position 1st day birth month: 23   09.6

Distance in month: 1   46.9

(Distance/number of days in month) *x*   (106.9)
number of birth date: (÷ 31 x 6)

Actual travel: 21.3

Starting position (1st day of birth month):   23 ♈ 09.6

+ actual travel: 21.3
(- *if retrograde*)

Position: 23♈ 30.9

⚸   ⊛   ☿ ⊗
(Diurnal charts - reverse for nocturnal)

Ascendant:	10 22 05		Ascendant:	10 22 05	
+ Moon	11 19 45		+ Sun	01 16 07	
	22 11 50			12 08 12	
- Sun	01 16 07		- Moon	11 19 45	
Position:	20 25 43			00 18 27	
	(08)				

⚸ = 25 ♏ 43   ⊗ = 18 ⋇ 27

83

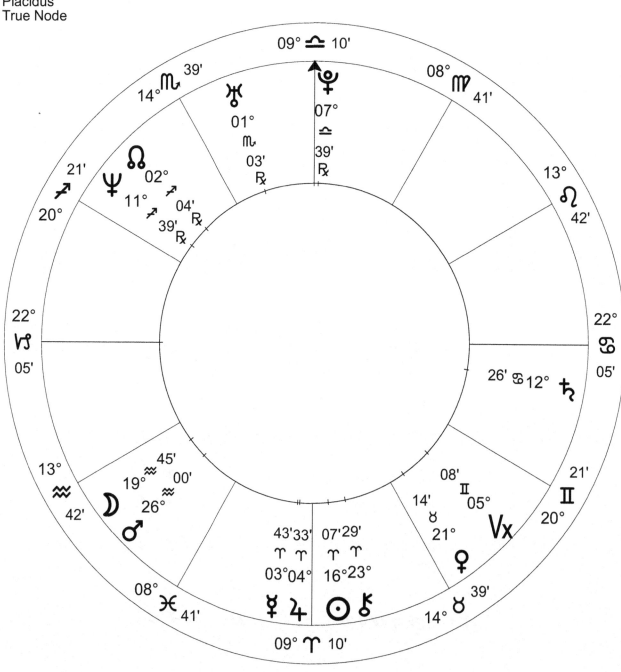

Kanga Roe
Natal Chart
Apr 6 1975, Sun
11:32 pm AEST -10:00
Sydney, Australia
33°S52' 151°E13'
Geocentric
Tropical
Placidus
True Node

Chapter 10

Calculating Progressions: Preliminary Steps

What are progressions?

Progressions are a symbolic advancement of the natal positions of the planets, the Midheaven and the Ascendant, used for the purpose of timing events in the subject's life, and detecting subtle modifications in the personality and outlook on life. The progressions we will be using are properly called secondary progressions. Secondary progressions use a 24-hour period of travel to represent one year of the subject's life. By way of contrast, tertiary progressions use the same 24-hour period to represent one month in the life. Tertiary progressions are little used today, but the methods of calculation given here can be used with modifications for tertiary progressions, substituting months for years, if desired.

The major alternative to secondary progressions is solar arc direction. Solar arc direction also uses a 24-hour period of travel to represent a year of life, but instead of using the actual travel of each planet in that period, adds to the earlier position of each planet either a flat rate of travel of one degree (the idealized diurnal motion of the Sun) or (the preferable method) the exact travel of the Sun for the 24-hour period (the solar arc). The disadvantage of the solar arc method is that, except for the Sun, the travel of the planets is notional rather than real. A positive aspect is that the outer planets travel much farther—using secondary progressions, the outer planets travel very little even over a lifetime. For this reason, solar arc directions are often useful in working with young subjects. However, in the system of secondary progressions, an event relating to an outer planet, such as a change of sign, or a change as between direct and retrograde motion, can be very significant. Both secondary progressions and solar arc directions derive from older systems of direction developed by Hellenistic astrologers. Some of these systems are quite complicated, though it seems that the concept of progression, as opposed to direction, is relatively modern.

We will provide some basic information about interpreting progressions in Chapter 14. But first, we are going to learn a number of techniques for calculating progressed events. These are:

- Calculation of progressed planetary positions for a given date and time;
- Calculation of the progressed Midheaven and Ascendant for the same date and time; and
- Calculation of the date and time at which a progressed planet will change sign, or contact a natal planet or other point in the natal chart.

Considerable precision is possible in progression calculations, and we will demonstrate the most precise techniques in each case. But bear in mind that, for all normal purposes, the precise time at which a progressed event occurs is probably unnecessary, and the date alone, rather than date and time, may suffice. Bear in mind also that the accuracy of a progressed chart depends on the accuracy of the natal chart, and the birth data. With any secondary chart, be it a progressed chart, a solar or lunar return, or a divisional chart, not only can the accuracy of such a chart never exceed that of the natal chart, but any error in the natal chart will be magnified in the secondary chart, in some cases to a very large extent.

Basic Information for Calculating Progressions

In order to calculate a progressed chart, you must, of course, have the subject's natal chart. If you have calculated the natal chart by hand, you should use the exact calculated values for the cusps of the Midheaven and Ascendant and the planetary positions, rather than the rounded-up values you copied on to the wheel. In the case of the cusps, convert any numbers after the decimal point to seconds by multiplying by 60. This will allow you a higher degree of precision. You must, of course, know the date and time for which the progressions are required. The preferred practice is to calculate progressions using the coordinates of the place of birth, rather than the place where the subject may currently be living, but if you prefer to relocate the chart, simply substitute the coordinates of the place of residence whenever necessary.

The mathematical techniques will almost all be familiar if you have mastered the principles of natal chart construction. They are, for the most part, the same, or easily recognizable variations. For this reason, do not attempt to learn to calculate progressions until you feel fairly comfortable with natal chart construction. When necessary, refer back to the earlier chapters of this book to refresh your memory about the techniques. Pencil, ruler and calculator will again be required, as will the ephemeris and tables of houses. We have supplied suggested work sheets, which we will use as we go along.

Figure 14, Leap Years			
1900	1940	1980	2020
1904	1944	1984	2024
1908	1948	1988	2028
1912	1952	1992	2032
1916	1956	1996	2036
1920	1960	2000	2040
1924	1964	2104	2044
1928	1968	2108	2048
1932	1972	2012	2052
1936	1976	2016	2056

The main technique is interpolation, which we have previously used in our natal house cusp and planetary position calculations. Because each period of 24 hours in the ephemeris represents one year for the purposes of progressions, we will be interpolating periods of 365 days, representing one year, and periods of 24 hours, depending on the calculation we are performing.

Figures 14 and 15 provide useful information. Figure 15 is a table assigning a number to each day of a standard year, beginning with 1 for January 1, and continuing numerically to December 31 (day 365). This table must be modified slightly if the year in question is a leap year, in which case February 29 is day 60, and 1 must be added to the numbers for all subsequent dates. A leap year is any even-numbered year whose digits are exactly divisible by 4, and, accordingly, every 4th year is a leap year. Figure 14 gives a list of leap years.

Calculating the Midnight Date and Time

The midnight date is crucial to progression calculations. It is called the midnight date because we are using a midnight ephemeris. The midnight date marks the beginning of a progressed year. It tells us what date of a year of the subject's life is represented by the position of a planet at midnight on a given ephemeris date. Once we know this, we can calculate on what subsequent date in the same year of life a progressed event occurs. For example, if midnight GMT on January 1 in the ephemeris represents September 10 in the year of life, then midnight GMT on January 2 will represent September 10 in the following year of life, and any ephemeris time in between the two midnights will yield an interpolated date in the year of life for any progressed event.

The availability of the midnight date method is the best of the several strong arguments for preferring a midnight ephemeris to a noon ephemeris. The midnight date is easy to calculate and always falls before the subject's date of birth. When calculating the equivalent "noon date," the date may fall before or after the birth date, according to the time of the subject's birth, and it is essential to remember whether to move forward or backward in the ephemeris.

The midnight ephemeris avoids this complication. The midnight time refines our calculations by providing, not only the date in the year of life, but the time on that date. Although the date alone will generally provide a sufficient approximation, the procedures using the time also are more precise, and quite straightforward.

We will illustrate our progression calculations by using Jane Doe's natal chart, so you will need to have this available. We will begin by calculating her midnight date. You will need to refer to the pages from the ephemeris. (Progressions Worksheet 1 is designed to be used for the midnight date/time calculation.)

Figure 15, Table of Numbers of Days in Standard Year

	Jan	Feb	Mar	Apr	May	Jun	Jul	Aug	Sept	Oct	Nov	Dec
1.	01	32	60	91	121	152	182	213	244	274	305	335
2.	02	33	61	92	122	153	183	214	245	275	306	336
3.	03	34	62	93	123	154	184	215	246	276	307	337
4.	04	35	63	94	124	155	185	216	247	277	308	338
5.	05	36	64	95	125	156	186	217	248	278	309	339
6.	06	37	65	96	126	157	187	218	249	279	310	340
7.	07	38	66	97	127	158	188	219	250	280	311	341
8.	08	39	67	98	128	159	189	220	251	281	312	342
9.	09	40	68	99	129	160	190	221	252	282	313	343
10.	10	41	69	100	130	161	191	222	253	283	314	344
11.	11	42	70	101	131	162	192	223	254	284	315	345
12.	12	43	71	102	132	163	193	224	255	285	316	346
13.	13	44	72	103	133	164	194	225	256	286	317	347
14.	14	45	73	104	134	165	195	226	257	287	318	348
15.	15	46	74	105	135	166	196	227	258	288	319	349
16.	16	47	75	106	136	167	197	228	259	289	320	350
17.	17	48	76	107	137	168	198	229	260	290	321	351
18.	18	49	77	108	138	169	199	230	261	291	322	352
19.	19	50	78	109	139	170	200	231	262	292	323	353
20.	20	51	79	110	140	171	201	232	263	293	324	354
21.	21	52	80	111	141	172	202	233	264	294	325	355
22.	22	53	81	112	142	173	203	234	265	295	326	356
23.	23	54	82	113	143	174	204	235	266	296	327	357
24.	24	55	83	114	144	175	205	236	267	297	328	358
25.	25	56	84	115	145	176	206	237	268	298	329	359
26.	26	57	85	116	146	177	207	238	269	299	330	360
27.	27	58	86	117	147	178	208	239	270	300	331	361
28.	28	59	87	118	148	179	209	240	271	301	332	362
29.	29		88	119	149	180	210	241	272	302	333	363
30.	30		89	120	150	181	211	242	273	303	334	364
31.	31		90		151		212	243	274	304		365

1. Note the sidereal time at midnight GMT on Jane's Greenwich birth date. Remember that, although her American birthday is May 20, 1945, her late evening birth resulted in a GMT time of 04 42 00 on the following day, May 21, 1945. Always use the sidereal time for midnight on the Greenwich birth date.

2. Deduct from this sidereal time Jane's GMT birth time. (If the birth time is greater than the sidereal time, remember that you can add 24 hours to the sidereal time, which is simply a revolving period of 24 hours). For the same reason, as well as to avoid a.m./p.m. errors, we will always use the 24-hour clock.

3. Add an acceleration of the birth time to the result. As in natal chart calculations, acceleration is an adjustment of 10 seconds per hour/1 second per 6 minutes, to the nearest second.

Thus, we have:

Sidereal Time midnight
GMT May 21, 1945:   15 53 05
- GMT birth time   04 42 00
                                   11 11 05
+ Acceleration of birth time: 47
                                   11 11 52

The result of this calculation will be the sidereal time on the midnight date. Look backwards from the birth date in the ephemeris until you come to it. Of course, it will almost always fall between the sidereal times for two consecutive days, in this case between March 10 and March 11, 1945. For approximate purposes (date only) we could simply select the date closer to the calculated sidereal time (March 11). But for more precise, work, we can calculate the time, as follows.

1. Note the midnight sidereal time on the later closest day, and that on the earlier closest day, and subtract to find the difference. Call this ST1.

2. Similarly, find the difference between our calculated sidereal time and the earlier closest time, and call this ST2.

3. The midnight time is then found by the formula [(ST2 / ST1) x 24] + midnight GMT on the earlier date.

Thus:

ST March 11:	11 13 09	Calc ST	11 11 52
ST March 10:	11 09 13	ST March 10: 11 09 13	
Difference	00 03 56 (ST1)		00 02 39 (ST2)

(Decimalizing) (2.65 / 3.93333) x 24 = 16.169503 = (reconverting) 16 10 10.

This period of time is added to midnight GMT on March 10. Thus, the midnight date/time is March 10, 1945, at 16 10 10 GMT.

Correlating Midnight Date/Time with Years of Life

Now that we have the midnight date and time, what does it mean? The midnight date and time represent the date in the year of life which is the equivalent of the progressed planetary positions at midnight GMT on the corresponding ephemeris date. Midnight on May 21, 1945, represents March 10 (at 16 10 10 GMT) in the year of birth (1945). Each successive midnight in the ephemeris represents March 10 (at the same time) in successive years. Thus ephemeris dates May 21-22, 1945 = year of life March 10, 1945–March 10, 1946; ephemeris dates May 22-23, 1945 = year of life March 10, 1946 - March 10, 1947, and so on.

It is worthwhile writing this correlation down on Progressions Worksheet 2, or, in pencil, on the margin of the ephemeris, because the choice of corresponding year is obviously crucial as we calculate progressed events. You may not find it necessary to write down every year. Intervals of, say, five years usually make it clear enough.

You will note that, because the midnight date always falls before the birth date, the first year of life begins before Jane was actually born. Do not worry about this. Remember that progressions are not transits; they are a symbolic, not a real advancement of the planetary positions, and we are simply correlating dates in the year to the interpolated time of birth.

Finally, one very important point. In Jane's case, the midnight date falls in the same year as her birth (1945). However, it is quite common, with a GMT birth time late in the day, for the midnight date to fall in the previous year. If this happens, do not panic. All it means is that midnight on the Greenwich birth date will correlate to the preceding calendar year. So, if this had happened in Jane's case, ephemeris date May 21, 1945, would have represented the midnight date in 1944, rather than 1945, and we would have had to correlate forward from 1944 instead of 1945. Always check to see whether the midnight date occurs in the same year as the birth or the previous year. Note this on your worksheet specifically. Obviously, there is potential for a serious error of one year in any later calculations unless we note this correctly and reflect it in our correlation. In Jane's case, a correlation at intervals of 5 years might look like this:

Date =	Year	Date =	Year	Date =	Year
May 21 =	1945	June 10 =	1965	June 30 =	1985
May 26 =	1950	June 15 =	1970	July 5 =	1990
May 31 =	1955	June 20 =	1975	July 10 =	1995
June 5 =	1960	June 25 =	1980	July 15 =	2000

Now we are ready to move ahead with the calculation of specific progressed events, beginning with the calculation of progressed planetary positions.

Chapter 11

Calculating Progressed Planetary Positions

Our first exercise is to calculate progressed planetary positions. Let us assume that we have been asked to calculate Jane Doe's progressed planetary positions for February 3, 1994, at 2:20 p.m. CST, which we will call the target date and time. Later, we will also calculate her progressed Midheaven and Ascendant for the target date and time. But, in contrast to natal chart construction, we begin with the planets, because the progressed Midheaven is calculated based on the position of the progressed Sun, and the progressed Ascendant, in turn, based on the progressed Midheaven.

The two essential pieces of information are the target date and time, and Jane's midnight date and time. The initial year of the midnight date (1945) is important only as the basis for the correlation with years of life, so, provided we have already noted this correctly, we need not repeat it. Each progressed year will begin on March 10. Because we are working with the midnight Greenwich ephemeris, we will begin by converting the target time to GMT expressed using the 24-hour clock system. 2:20 p.m. CST converts to 8:20 p.m. or 20 20 00 GMT. Note this information on Progressions Worksheet 3, as follows:

Midnight date/time: March 10, at 16 10 10 GMT

Target date/time: February 3, 1994, at 20 20 00 GMT

Finding the Ephemeris Dates Corresponding to the Target Year

Our target date falls in the year 1994. Our first task is to determine, using our correlation of ephemeris dates and years of life, which ephemeris dates to use as the basis of the progressed planetary positions. Bear in mind that the year aways begins with March 10, so our target date falls between March 10, 1993, and March 10, 1994. Using our correlations (worksheet 2) we can see that the year 1993 is represented by ephemeris date July 8, 1945, and 1994 by July 9, 1945. Therefore, the positions of the planets at midnight GMT on those dates will be our starting point (see Figure 21, previous chapter).

Finding the Distance Between Midnight Date and Target Date

Because one 24-hour period in the ephemeris corresponds with one year of life beginning on March 10, we will always begin by finding how many days separate the target date from the previous midnight date. This will tell us what proportion of the year has elapsed at the target date, and, from this, we will be able to interpolate the travel of each planet as the same proportion of the 24-hour ephemeris period between midnight GMT on July 8 and July 9, 1945. For greater accuracy, we can also find the number of hours, minutes and seconds which have elapsed.

The simplest way to calculate the distance is to use the numbers assigned to each day in the table of numbers (fig.19, previous chapter). As 1994 was not a leap year, we can take the numbers as written. March 10 is day 69, and February 3 is day 34. Note these numbers on your worksheet. Where the two dates fall in the same calendar year, calculating the distance is a simple matter of subtraction. In this case, however, we are finding the distance between March 10, 1993, and February 3, 1994. The procedure here is to find the difference between the two, and then deduct the result from 365 days, as follows. (Note that we are using the times also, but whole days can be used for less precise purposes).

	Day #	Time (GMT)
March 10:	69	16 10 10
February 3:	34	20 20 00
	34	19 50 10
	365	00 00 00
	-34	19 50 10
Elapsed days/time:	330	04 09 50

As in the case of natal chart construction, this elapsed time will be our multiplier for interpolation, so we must decimalize it. The procedure for this should already be familiar. Remember, however that there are 24 hours in a day, so, when we get to the 4 hours, we will divide by 24, rather than 60. So, the procedure will be:

1. Divide the seconds by 60. 50 / 60 = 0.83333. So we have 9.83333 minutes,

2. Divide 9.83333 by 60 = 0.16388. So we have 4.16388 hours.

3. Divide 4.16388 by 24 = 0.17349. Therefore, our multiplier (the number of days) will be 330.17349.

Calculating the Progressed Planetary Positions

Now, we will proceed exactly as we did in natal chart construction. Let us take the Sun as an example. We will: (1) note the positions of the Sun at midnight GMT on July 9 and July 8, 1945; (2) find the total travel for the 24-hour period; (3) interpolate by dividing the travel by 365 and multiplying by 330.17349; and (4) add the interpolated travel to the earlier position. (If we were dealing with a retrograde planet, we would subtract instead of adding.)

Position of Sun on July 9:	16 ♋ 24 27
Position of Sun on July 8:	15 27 33
Total travel:	56 54 (= 56.9)

(56.9 / 365) x 330.17349 = 51.47087
(Reconverting to minutes/seconds by multiplying 0.47087 by 60) = 51 28

Position on July 8:	15 ♋ 27 33
+ actual travel:	51 28
Position of progressed Sun:	16 ♋ 19 01

As another example, let us calculate the position of the progressed Moon. As in natal chart construction, because of her far greater diurnal motion, the potential for error is greater in the case of the Moon than in that of any other planet. And here, we want to remind you of a technique for dealing with potential sign changes. This can happen with any planet, but happens more often with the Moon. Moreover, a change of sign by a progressed planet is always an important event, so this technique will frequently be useful. It is very simple. It is awkward to try to subtract from, say, 1 degree of the next sign. There are 30 degrees in a sign, so 1 degree of the next sign can equally well be expressed as 31 degrees of the last sign, making subtraction much easier. For example, instead of writing 1 degree of Gemini, we could write 31 degrees of Taurus, making an earlier position in Taurus easy to deal with. In the example below, the position of the Moon at midnight GMT on July 9 is actually 9 4 10 06, but because the earlier position falls in Gemini, we have written the July 9 position as 39 3 10 06. If the answer comes to more than 30 degrees, we will know that the progressed Moon is in Cancer.

Position of Moon on July 9:	39 ♊ 10 06	
Position of Moon on July 8:	25 13 39	
Total travel:	13 56 27	(= 13.94083)

(13.94083 / 365) x 330.17349 = 12.61064 = 12 36 38

Position on July 8:	25 ♊ 13 39
+ actual travel:	12 36 38
Position of progressed Moon:	37 3 50 17 = 7 ♋ 50 17

The remaining planetary positions are calculated in exactly the same way. Of course, with practice, it will be quite easy to "ballpark" the positions of the outer planets, as in the case of natal chart work. Our calculations for Mercury, Venus and Mars are as follows:

	☿	♀	♂
July 9:	8 ♌ 47.0	1 ♊ 21.7	19 ♉ 57.4
July 8:	7 13.0		0 19.7
Total travel:	1 34.0	1 02.0	42.5

(/ 365) x 330.17349

	1 25.0	56.0	38.4

	☿	♀	♂
July 8:	7 ♌ 13.0	0 ♊ 19.7	19 ♉ 14.9
+ actual travel:	1 25.0	56.0	38.4
Progressed:	8 ♌ 38.0	1 ♊ 15.7	19 ♉ 53.3

It is usual to write the progressed planetary positions on a wheel outside the natal chart, so that the aspects between the natal and progressed planets, and the houses in which the progressed planets fall, can easily be observed. Round the progressed positions up or down to the nearest minute, as in the case of the natal planets.

Chapter 12

Calculating the Progressed Midheaven and Ascendant

The Progressed Midheaven

The calculation of the progressed Midheaven is a simple procedure. The information required is the position of the natal Sun, the natal Midheaven, and the progressed Sun. The procedure is set out on the lower half of worksheet 2. It is to find the distance between the progressed Sun and the natal Sun (the solar arc) and add this distance to the natal Midheaven. The result will be the progressed Midheaven. Remember to use the precise, calculated positions of the progressed Sun, the natal Sun and the natal Midheaven, not the rounded-off values written on the wheel. There may be one or more signs between the progressed and natal positions of the Sun, so it may be easier to express the progressed Sun as more than 30 degrees of the natal sign, or express both positions as so many degrees from 0 Aries. We used the former technique in the last chapter in calculating the position of the progressed Moon. The latter is illustrated below. We will calculate Jane Doe's progressed Midheaven for the same target date and time (February 3, 1994, at 20 20 00 GMT).

(Degrees from 0 Aries)

Progressed Sun:	16 ♋ 19 01	106 19 01
- Natal Sun:	29 ♉ 45 39	59 45 39
Solar arc:		46 33 22

Natal MC:	3 ♏ 27 58
+ solar arc	46 33 22
Progressed MC =	50 ♏ 01 20 = 20 ♐ 01 20

The Progressed Ascendant

The progressed Ascendant is based on the position of the progressed Midheaven. The procedure appears more complicated, but is actually substantially the same as the procedure for calculating the natal Ascendant. The difference is that, instead of arriving at the correct columns in the tables of houses by calculating the sidereal time, in this case, we use the two columns which have the Midheaven closest to the progressed Midheaven. The procedure is set out on Worksheet 5.

We will need the following information:

1. The progressed Midheaven: 20 ♐ 01 20.

2. The closest earlier and later Midheavens in the tables of houses. In this case, these are 19 ♐ 53 and 20 ♐ 49.

3. The latitude factor. As we know from our natal chart construction, this factor is the minutes/seconds of the latitude of the place of birth divided by 60. The minutes/seconds of latitude of Austin are 16 01, producing a LF of 0.26694. We will also need the closest lower and higher latitudes, in this case 30 and 31.

Note all this on your worksheet. The procedure is now as follows:

1. Find the difference between the closest earlier and closest later values for the Midheaven. Call this D1.

2. Find the difference between the progressed Midheaven and the closest earlier midheaven. Call this D2.

3. Using the lower latitude (30) find the Ascendants corresponding to the closest earlier and later Midheavens, and find the difference between them. Call this D3.

4. Perform the calculation (D2 / D1) x D3, and call the result D4.

5. Add D4 to the minutes of the Ascendant corresponding to the closest earlier Midheaven. The result will be the unadjusted Ascendant.

6. Last, perform a latitude adjustment, exactly as in the case of the natal Ascendant. Using the earlier sidereal time, find the ascendants for the higher and lower latitudes, and the difference between the two. Multiply the difference by the LF. Add the result to or subtract the result from the minutes of the unadjusted Ascendant, using the formula: if higher is higher, add, if lower is higher, subtract. (If you have become unclear about this, you might want to review the corresponding natal chart section). In Jane's case, our calculation is as follows:

Closest later MC:	20 ♐ 49	
Closest earlier MC:	19 __ 53__	
Difference:	56 (D1)	

Progressed MC:	20 ♐ 01 20	
Closest earlier MC:	19 __ 53 00__	
Difference:	08 20 (D2)	
(= 8.33333)		

At latitude 30:

Later Asc:	15 ♓ 33	
Earlier Asc:	14 __ 07__	
Difference:	01 26 (D3) (= 86)	

D4 = (D2 / D1) x D3 = (8.33333 / 56) x 86 = 12.7976

Earlier Asc:	14 ♓ 07
+ D4	__12.7976__
Unadjusted Asc =	14 ♓ 19.7976

Using earlier sidereal time:

Asc at higher lat:	13 ♓ 55
Asc at lower lat:	14 __ 07__
Difference:	12 x LF (0.26694) = 3.20328

Unadjusted Asc:	14 ♓ 19.7976
(lower is higher)	- __03.20328__
Progressed Asc =	14 ♓ 16.59432

Lastly, the progressed Midheaven and Ascendant may be rounded up or down and copied on to the outer wheel. It is not usual to calculate other progressed house cusps, but, if desired, the same method can be used, based on the progressed Midheaven.

Progressed Ascendant in Southern Hemisphere Charts

If you are calculating a progressed chart for a location in the southern hemisphere, using a table of houses for northern latitudes, it is necessary to make an adjustment to the method described above. This consists of reversing cusps twice, as follows.

1. Calculate the progressed midheaven exactly as shown earlier in this chapter. But then take the point opposite as the Midheaven for the purpose of calculating the progressed Ascendant, e.g. if the calculated progressed Midheaven is 3 ♈ 16, take a Midheaven of 3 ♎ 16 as your starting point.

2. Perform the progressed Ascendant calculation exactly as shown above, but reverse the final cusp, e.g. if the calculated progressed Ascendant is 18 ♐ 06, this will be the cusp of the progressed seventh house; the progressed Ascendant will be 18 ♊ 06.

Overleaf is Jane's progressed chart for our target date and time calculated using a computer program, and written outside her natal chart.

Jane Doe
Natal Chart
May 20 1945, Sun
11:42 pm CWT +5:00
Austin, TX
30°N16'01" 097°W44'34"
Geocentric
Tropical
Placidus
True Node

Outer Wheel
Jane Doe
Sec.Prog. SA in Long
Feb 3 1994, Thu
2:20 pm CWT +5:00
Austin, TX
30°N16'01" 097°W44'34"
Geocentric
Tropical
Placidus
True Node

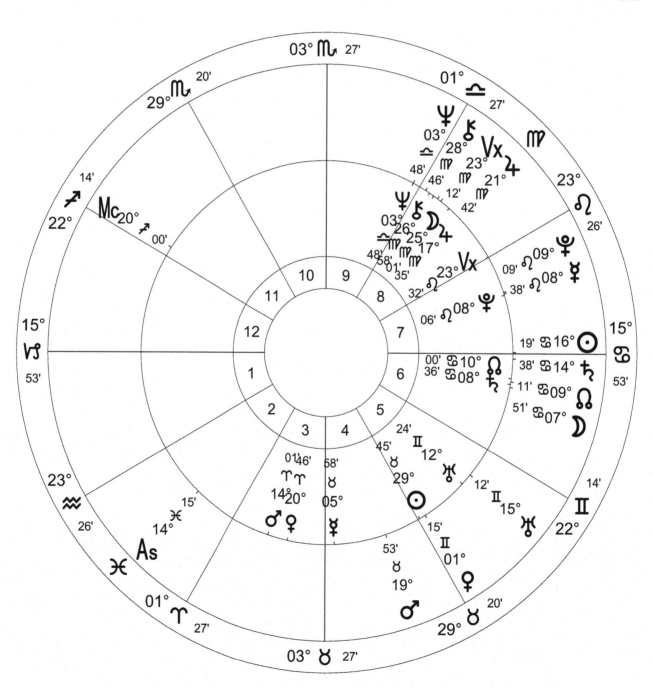

Chapter 13

Calculating the Date and Time
of Progressed Contacts

In this chapter, we will calculate the date and time at which a progressed planet reaches a target position, for example the beginning of a new sign, a natal house cusp, or first forms a conjunction or aspect with a natal planet or a point such as the natal Ascendant. What we are doing here is, in a sense, the reverse of finding the progressed planetary positions, where the date and time were a given, and we were finding the corresponding positions. Here, we are told the position, and we have to find the date and time. Nonetheless, the method is more or less the same. It is still a process of interpolation. The procedure is set out on Worksheet 4. We will take a number of examples based on Jane Doe's calculated natal chart. You will need to refer to the relevant pages of the ephemeris (Figure 21). As always, you should also note Jane's midnight date and time on your worksheet: March 10, at 16 10 10 GMT.

Progressed Sign Changes

As our first example, let us assume that we have been asked to calculate the date and time at which Jane's progressed Sun first entered Cancer. We know that this must have occurred at some point during a year of life beginning on March 10. The first task is to determine which year. Looking at the relevant page of the ephemeris, we see that the Sun entered Cancer between Midnight GMT on June 21 and midnight GMT on June 22, 1945, during which time it moved from 29 ♊ 15 00 to 0 ♋ 12 14. Looking at our correlation to years of life (worksheet 2) we find that these two ephemeris dates represent progressed years 1976 and 1977. Therefore, Jane's progressed Sun entered Cancer sometime during the year of life between March 10, 1976, and March 10, 1977.

Note also that 1976 was a leap year. Therefore, the number for any date after February 28 in that year, including March 10, must be increased by one. Thus, March 10 will be day 70, not 69. (This is not true, however, of dates in 1977).

There are two equally good methods of performing a progressed sign change calculation.

First Method: In this method, we use the planetary positions as shown in the ephemeris (above) and interpolate from them. The method is as follows.

1. Note the position of the Sun at midnight GMT on the later date (June 22) and the earlier date (June 21) and find the total travel for that period. Call this T1. (Hint: as in our previous examples which involved sign changes, make use of the technique of calling 0 degrees of Cancer 30 degrees of Gemini. Not only is it easier, but, in this case, it avoids having to write the glyphs in the calculations.)

2. Find the travel between the position on the earlier day and the target position, and call this T2. As we are

asked to find when the progressed Sun first entered Cancer, the target position is 0 ♋ 00, though we are going to express it as 30 ♊ 00.

3. To find the number of days it took the progressed Sun to reach the target position, perform the calculation (T2 / T1) x 365. Use any numbers after the decimal point to calculate the time. By adding the result to the midnight date/time, we arrive at the date and time when the progressed Sun entered Cancer. If the number of days in the answer is greater than 365, this indicates that the date falls in the later year. Deduct 365 to find the number of the day.

Our calculation should look like this:

Position later day:	30 12 14	Target position:	30 00 00
Position earlier day:	29 15 00	Position earlier day:	29 15 00
Travel:	57 14		45 00
	(T1)		(T2)

(T2 / T1) x 365 = 286.98311 = 286 days, 23 hours, 35 minutes, 41 seconds.

Midnight Date: Day 70 at 16 10 10 (GMT)

+   286   23 35 41

=   Day 357 at 15 45 51 (GMT) = December 22, 1976, at 15 45 51 (GMT)

Second Method: In this method, we make use of the fact that the ephemeris records the date and time of planetary ingresses into a sign, so we interpolate from this information, taking the time of the ingress as a fraction of 24 hours, and expressing the result as a proportion of 365 days. The ephemeris tells us that the Sun entered Cancer on June 21 at 18:52 (GMT). Decimalized, this equates to 18.86666. Therefore, the number of days elapsed during the progressed year = (18.86666 / 24) x 365 = 286.93055, which, with a negligible discrepancy, is the number we arrived at by the first method. The discrepancy is caused by the fact that the ephemeris records the time of the event in hours and minutes only. We can now complete the calculation in the same way.

This method is available only for events of which the precise time is given in the ephemeris. It can be used to determine progressed lunations (later, this chapter). It can also be used to determine the date/time when a planet stationed, went retrograde, or returned to direct motion by progression.

Now we will do a second example using the progressed Moon, and assume we have been asked to find the date on which Jane's progressed Moon most recently entered Taurus. The reason for the words "most recently" is that the progressed Moon takes only approximately 29 years (ephemeris days) to orbit the zodiac, so that within a normal life span, the progressed Moon can enter any given sign on 2 or possibly 3 occasions. This is in contrast to the other planets, in which a change of sign by progression is such a rare event that a planet will not enter the same new sign more than once in one lifetime by simple direct motion. (Mercury will occasionally do so by entering a sign, retrograding back into the previous sign, then going direct and entering the new sign again. But this is a function of Mercury's speed and relatively short retrograde periods.)

First method: Looking at the relevant page of the ephemeris, we see that the progressed Moon most recently (this is being written in 1997) entered Taurus between midnight GMT on July 4 (when its position was 28 1 10) and midnight GMT on July 5, 1945 (12 2 29 49). Looking at our correlation to years of life, we see that these ephemeris dates correspond to 1989 and 1990. Therefore, the progressed Moon entered Taurus at some time between March 10, 1989, and March 10, 1990. As 1989 was not a leap year, the midnight date is day 69. We then proceed in exactly the same way as in the case of the progressed Sun. Our same-sign technique means we will write 12 2 as 42 1, which looks rather strange, but, again, is most definitely the easiest way to handle this.

Position later day:	42 29 49	Target position:	30 00 00
Position earlier day:	28 10 00	Position earlier day:	28 10 00
Travel:	14 19 49		01 50 00
	(T1)		(T2)

(T2 / T1) x 365 = 46.69602 = 46 days, 16 hours, 42 minutes, 17 seconds

Midnight date:	Day 69 at 16 10 10 (GMT)
+	46 16 42 17
=	Day 116 at 08 52 27 (GMT) = April 26, 1989, at 08 52 27 (GMT)

Second method: From the ephemeris, we see that the Moon entered Taurus at 03:04 GMT (=3.06666) on July 4, 1945. Thus, the number of elapsed days = (3.06666/24) x 365 = 46.63888, which will give approximately the same result as the first method.

Last, an example using a planet whose movement is recorded in the ephemeris using only degrees and minutes (decimalized). Let us assume we have been asked to find the date and time at which progressed Venus enters Gemini. Looking at the ephemeris and our correlations, we determine that this event occurred between March 10, 1992, and March 10, 1993. 1992 was a leap year.

Position later day:	30 19.7	Target position:	30 00.0
Position earlier day:	29 18.1	Position earlier day:	29 18.1
Travel:	01 01.6		41.9
	(T1)		(T2)

(T2 / T1) x 365 = 248.2711 = 248 days, 6 hours, 30 minutes, 23 seconds

Midnight date:	Day 70 at 16 10 10 (GMT)
+	248 06 30 23
=	Day 318 at 22 40 33 (GMT) = November 14, 1992, at 22 40 33 (GMT)

Progressed Contacts with Planets or Points in Natal Chart

Another very useful kind of information is the date and time at which a progressed planet contacts, or forms an aspect with a planet or point in the natal chart. The technique for determining this is exactly the same as that given above. In this case, the target position is the position of the natal planet or point. Remember to use the calculated position of this planet or point, rather than the rounded-off position you copied on to the wheel. Let us assume we have been asked to determine the date and time at which Jane's progressed Moon most recently (as of 1997) entered her natal twelfth house. Our target position, the calculated twelfth house cusp, is 22 ♐ 15.21926, which converts to 22 ♐ 15 13. Looking at the ephemeris, we see that the progressed Moon reached that position sometime between midnight GMT on June 24 and 25, 1945, and these dates correlate to 1979 and 1980. Therefore, the event occurred between March 10, 1979, and March 10, 1980.

Position later day:	25 38 41	Target position:	22 15 13
Position earlier day:	13 06 35	Position earlier day:	13 06 35
Travel:	12 32 06		09 08 38
	(T1)		(T2)

(T2 / T1) x 365 = 266.256 = 266 days, 6 hours, 8 minutes, 38 seconds

Midnight date:	Day 69 at 16 10 10 (GMT)
+	266 at 06 08 38
=	Day 335 at 22 18 48 (GMT) = December 1, 1979, at 22 18 48 (GMT)

Now assume we have been asked to determine when, after this event, the progressed Moon conjuncts natal Mars. Our target position is the calculated position of natal Mars, which is 14 ♈ 01.31. Because, in the case of the Moon, we are working with degrees, minutes, and seconds, it is convenient to convert the minutes of Mars' position to minutes and seconds. The minutes are 01.31, which converts to 01 18. Looking at the ephemeris, we see that, after the last event, the progressed Moon reaches this position sometime between midnight GMT on July 3 and 4, 1945, and these dates correlate to 1988 and 1989. Therefore, the event occurred between March 10, 1988, and March 10, 1989. 1988 was a leap year.

Position later day:	28 10 00	Target position:	14 01 18
Position earlier day:	13 53 26	Position earlier day:	13 53 26
Travel:	14 16 34		00 07 52
	(T1)		(T2)

(T2 / T1) x 365 = 3.35212 = 3 days, 8 hours, 27 minutes, 3 seconds

Midnight date:	Day 70 at 16 10 10 (GMT)
+	03 08 27 03
=	Day 74 at 00 37 13 (GMT) = March 15, 1988, at 00 37 13 (GMT)

Progressed Lunations

A progressed lunation occurs when the progressed Sun and Moon are conjunct (a progressed new Moon) or opposite (a progressed full Moon). These are significant events, and we may wish to calculate the date and time of such a progressed lunation. We begin by establishing the date and time of the actual lunation, and then, as always, interpolate this to a date and time in the corresponding year of life. To calculate the time of a lunation mathematically is extremely complicated, and, mercifully, unnecessary. The ephemeris records the date and GMT time of each lunation in the tables at the foot of each page, so we can use what we have been calling the second method.

Let us assume we have been asked to find the date and time of Jane's progressed full Moon in Capricorn. There will be only one such lunation in her lifetime, and by looking at the ephemeris, we determine that the actual lunation occurred at 3 0 40 on June 25, 1945, at 15 08 GMT. This lunation occurred between midnight GMT on June 25 and June 26, 1945, which correlates to the years 1980 and 1981. Therefore, the progressed lunation occurred between March 10, 1980, and March 10, 1981. 1980 was a leap year. The remaining information, in this kind of case, is given to us. The interpolation will be time of the lunation as a proportion of 24 hours. So, to obtain the number of days to add to the midnight date, we perform the calculation (time of lunation / 24) x 365. Our calculation will be as follows.

Time of lunation: 15 08 00 (GMT)
(= 15.13333)

(15.13333 / 24) x 365 = 230.15275 = 230 days, 03 hours, 40 minutes

Midnight date:	Day 70 at 16 10 10 (GMT)
+	230 03 40 00
=	Day 300 at 19 50 10 (GMT) = October 27, 1980, at 19 50 10 (GMT)

Progressed Changes of Motion

Because the ephemeris records the time at which a planet, having stationed, changes from direct to retrograde motion or vice versa, it is a simple matter to calculate the date and time of a progressed change of motion, using our second method. Progressed changes of motion can be very significant for interpretive purposes—see Erin Sullivan's masterly treatment of them in *Retrograde Planets: Traversing the Lunar Landscape* (Arkana, 1992).

Let us calculate the date and time at which Jane Doe's Neptune turned direct by progression. From the ephemeris, we see that this event occurred in actuality on June 14, 1945, at 18:38 GMT. From our correlation, we see that this corresponds to the actual year of life March 10, 1969 to March 10, 1970. Our calculation will be as follows:

Time of station/direct = 18:38 (= 18.63333)
(18.63333 / 24) x 365 = 283.38194 = 283 days, 9 hours, 10 minutes

Midnight date = Day   69 at 16 10 10 (GMT)
+   283   09 10 00
=   Day 353 at 01 20 10 = December 19, 1969, at 01 20 10 GMT

Now, we have provided a number of practice exercises, based on the calculated natal charts of Richard Roe, Mary Moe, Wong Doe, and Kanga Roe. The relevant pages of the ephemeris and tables of houses are provided. The answers to the problems set are also given, using our worksheets. Try your hand at these and other problems until you feel comfortable with the techniques. As in the case of natal chart construction, do not worry about making mistakes—they are inevitable, and make for good learning experiences. And always remember—practice makes perfect!

Progressions: Practice Exercises

Richard Roe

Using Richard Roe's calculated natal chart:

1. Calculate progressed planetary positions, Midheaven, and Ascendant for March 8, 1995, at 4:18 a.m. PST.
2. At what date and time did Richard's progressed Sun enter Sagittarius?
3. What are the date and time of Richard's progressed Full Moon in Gemini?
4. At what date and time does Richard's progressed Moon first conjunct natal Neptune?

Mary Moe

Using Mary Moe's calculated natal chart:

1. Calculate progressed planetary positions, Midheaven, and Ascendant for November 19, 1996, at 3:42 p.m. CST.
2. At what date and time did Mary's progressed Sun enter Cancer?
3. What are the date and time of Mary's progressed Full Moon in Capricorn?
4. At what date and time does Mary's progressed Moon conjunct her natal Ascendant for the second time?

Wong Doe

Using Wong Doe's calculated natal chart:

1. Calculate progressed planetary positions, Midheaven, and Ascendant for April 20, 1997, at 11:37 a.m. GMT.
2. At what date and time does Wong's progressed Moon first conjunct his natal IC?
3. At what date and time does Wong's progressed Mars enter Aquarius?
4. At what date and time does Wong's progressed Moon first enter Aquarius?

Kanga Roe

Using Kanga Roe's calculated natal chart:

1. Calculate progressed planetary positions, Midheaven, and Ascendant for August 18, 1995, at 7:22 p.m. AEST.
2. At what date and time does Kanga's progressed Sun enter Taurus?
3. At what date and time does Kanga's progressed Moon first enter Cancer?
4. What are the date and time of Kanga's progressed Full Moon in Scorpio?

The completed Worksheets and computer-calculated charts are on the following pages.

PROGRESSIONS WORKSHEET 1

Name: RICHARD ROE

Date and Time of Birth (at Greenwich): NOVEMBER 5, 1980 22:15 GMT

Midnight Date Calculation

Sidereal time at midnight Greenwich for *Greenwich* birth date:	02	57	30
- Birth time (GMT):	22	15	00
	04	42	30
+ acceleration of birth time: (10 secs/hour, 1 sec/6 mins.):		3	42
Sidereal time for birth (STB) =	04	46	12

Midnight date = closest earlier ST = DEC. 3   Same / (previous) year? (1979)

Time:

ST later day: 4 48 51   STB: 4 46 12

- ST earlier day: 4 44 55   - ST earlier day: 4 44 55

        03 56 (ST1)   1 17 (ST2)
        3.93333   1.28333

Time = [(ST2 / ST1) x 24] + midnight, earlier date =

= 7.83051 HOURS

= 7 49 50 GMT

RICHARD ROE   **PROGRESSIONS WORKSHEET 2**

Correlation of years with dates
(Greenwich birth date = year in which midnight date falls, then 1 day = 1 year)

Date	=	Year		Date	=	Year		Date	=	Year

(1980)

Nov 5 = 1979

Nov 10 = 1984

Nov 15 = 1989

Nov 20 = 1994

Nov 25 = 1999

Calculation of progressed MC

MARCH 8, 1995   04:18 PST

Progressed Sun: 28 ♏ 05 18

- Natal Sun: 13 ♏ 39 29

Solar arc =   14   25   49

+ Natal MC   21 ♐ 33 41

Prog MC =   35 ♐ 59 30 = 5 ♑ 59 30

108

MARCH 8, 1995 AT 4:18 PST = 12:18 GMT

RICHARD ROE   **PROGRESSIONS WORKSHEET 3**
Progressed planetary positions for target date/time

Target date = Day # 67 + 365 = 432   Midnight date = Day # 337
Time 12 18 00 (GMT) 432 12 18 00   Time 07 49 50 (GMT)
                     -337 07 49 50

Difference (n) =   95 04 28 10   (Decimalized = 95.18622)

	☉	☽
Position on later year day:	28 ♏ 50 05	10 ♈ 48 51
Position on earlier year day:	27 49 31	26 42 06
Travel:	1 00 34	15 06 45
[(Travel/365) x n] =	15 47	3 56 28
+ position on earlier day:	27 ♏ 49 31	25 ♈ 42 06
Position on target date=	28 ♏ 05 18	29 ♈ 38 34

	☿	♀	♂
Position on later year day:	9 ♏ 25.7	26 ♎ 13.7	29 ♐ 11.4
Position on earlier year day: (Reverse if ℞)	8 21.7	25 00.0	28 26.1
Travel:	1 04.0	1 13.7	45.3
[(Travel/365) x n} =	16.7	19.2	11.8
+ position on earlier day: (- if ℞)	8 ♏ 21.7	25 ♎ 00.0	28 ♐ 26.1
Position on target date =	8 ♏ 33.4	25 ♎ 19.2	28 ♐ 37.9

RICHARD ROE   **PROGRESSIONS WORKSHEET 4**

To find date/time progressed planet reaches target position – PROG. ☉
ENTERS ♐

Midnight date = Day # 338 *   Time: 07 49 50 GMT

* LEAP YEAR
Target between midnight date __1996__ (earlier year) and __1997__ (later year)

Position on later day: 30 51 18   Target Position: 30 00 00

-Position on earlier day: 29 50 41   -Position on earlier day: 29 50 41

Travel (T1):   1 00 37   Travel (T2):   09 19

(If B, T1 = earlier-later, T2 = earlier-target)

[(T2 / T1) x 365] =   56 02 23 44   (Days/time)

+ midnight date/time: 338   07 49 50 GMT

Target date/time =   394
                    -365
                     29 10 13 34 GMT (JANUARY 29, 1997)

To find date of progressed lunation

Date of lunation: NOV 22 Day #   Degree of lunation: 0 ♊ 07
Time of lunation 06 39 (GMT)
Midnight date = Day # 338 * Time: 07 49 50 GMT

* LEAP YEAR
Target between midnight date __1996__ (earlier year) and __1997__ (later year)

(Time of lunation / 24) x 365 = 101 03 15 00   (Days/time)

+ midnight date/time: 338 07 49 50

Date/time of prog. lunation = 439
                              -365
                               74 11 04 50 = MARCH 15, 1997

Murphy & Koch, The Math of Chart Construction (AFA)

110

RICHARD ROE   **PROGRESSIONS WORKSHEET 4**   PROG. D ♂
                                                        NATAL Ψ
To find date/time progressed planet reaches target position FOR FIRST TIME

Midnight date = Day # **338** *   Time: **07 49 50 GMT**

　* LEAP YEAR
Target between midnight date _**1984**_ (earlier year) and _**1985**_ (later year)

Position on later day:　**23 41 07**   Target Position:　**21 ◟ 01 24**

-Position on earlier day: **11 25 20**   -Position on earlier day: **11 25 20**

Travel (T1):　**12 15 47**   Travel (T2):　**9 36 04**
　　　　　(.26305)   **(.60111)**
(If B, T1 = earlier-later, T2 = earlier-target)

[(T2 / T1) x 365) =　**285 18 28 04**   (Days/time)

+ midnight date/time: **338 07 49 50 GMT**

Target date/time =　**624**
　　　　　　　　-365
　　　　　　　　259 02 17 54 = SEPTEMBER 16, 1985
To find date of progressed lunation

Date of lunation:　　Day #　　　　　Degree of lunation:
Time of lunation　　　(GMT)
Midnight date = Day #　　Time:

Target between midnight date _____(earlier year) and _____ (later year)

(Time of lunation / 24) x 365 =　　　　　　(Days/time)

+ midnight date/time:

　　　　　　　　_____
Date/time of prog. lunation =

MARCH 8, 1995 4:18 PST

RICHARD ROE   **PROGRESSIONS WORKSHEET 5**
                     Calculation of progressed Asc

Progressed MC = 5 ♑ 59 30 *Southern hemisphere, reverse =*
Closest MCs in table houses to prog MC = earlier: 5 ♑ 30   later: 6 ♑ 26
Distance earlier - later =   56   mins. (D1)
Distance earlier- prog MC = 29 30 mins. (D2)

Using lower latitude: (34)   LF = 0.05083
Asc for later sidereal time: 10 ♈ 45

Asc for earlier sidereal time: 9 ♈ 13

Distance in mins. (D3) =   1   32   (92)

(D2 / D1) x D3 =   (D4)
        48.46428
Asc for earlier sidereal time: 9 ♈ 13
+ D4
                                    48.46428
Unadjusted Asc =   10 ♈ 01.46428

Using earlier sidereal time:
Asc at higher lat: 9 ♈ 22
Asc at lower lat: 9 ♈ 13
Distance in mins =   09
x latitude factor
(mins of lat/60) =   0.45747   (latitude correction)

Unadjusted Asc: 10 ♈ 01.46428

+/- Lat corr:
 (if higher is higher, add)   00.45747

Prog Asc =   10 ♈ 01.92175 *(Southern hemisphere, reverse)*

112

Inner Wheel
Richard Roe
Natal Chart
Nov 5 1980, Wed
2:15 pm PST +8:00
Los Angeles, CA
34°N03'08" 118°W14'34"
Geocentric
Tropical
Placidus
True Node

Outer Wheel
Richard Roe
Sec.Prog. SA in Long
Mar 8 1995, Wed
2:20 pm PST +8:00
Los Angeles, CA
34°N03'08" 118°W14'34"
Geocentric
Tropical
Placidus
True Node

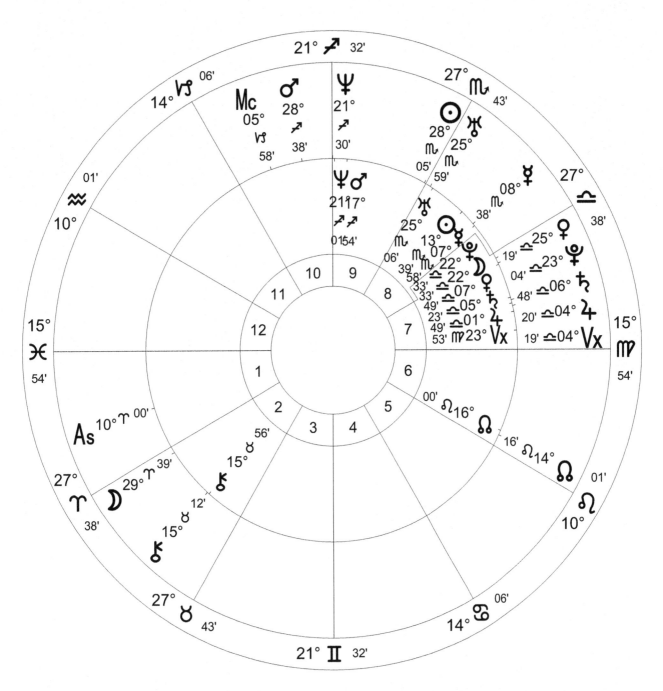

113

PROGRESSIONS WORKSHEET 1

Name: MARY MOE

Date and Time of Birth (at Greenwich): JUNE 11, 1965   04 25 00 GMT

Midnight Date Calculation

Sidereal time at midnight Greenwich
for *Greenwich* birth date: 17 16 29

- Birth time (GMT):   04 25 00
                                                    ─────────────
                                                          12 51 29

+ acceleration of birth time:
(10 secs/hour, 1 sec/6 mins.):   44
                                                    ─────────────
Sidereal time for birth (STB) =   12 52 13

Midnight date = closest earlier ST = APRIL 4/5 (Same)/ previous year?

Time:
    ST later day: 12 52 20   STB: 12 52 13

   - ST earlier day: 12 48 24   - ST earlier day: 12 48 24
                    ──────────   ──────────
                       3 56 (ST1)   3 49 (ST2)

Time = [(ST2 / ST1) x 24] + midnight, earlier date = APRIL 4, 1965 = DAY 94

                                             AT   23 17 17 GMT

MARY MOE   **PROGRESSIONS WORKSHEET 2**

Correlation of years with dates
(Greenwich birth date = year in which midnight date falls, then 1 day = 1 year)

Date = Year   Date = Year   Date = Year

(1965)

June 11 = 1965   July 6 = 1990

June 16 = 1970   July 11 = 1995

June 21 = 1975   July 16 = 2000

June 26 = 1980

July 1 = 1985

Calculation of progressed MC   NOVEMBER 19, 1996
                                    21 42 00 GMT

Progressed Sun: 20 ♋ 02 16

- Natal Sun: 20 ♊ 02 08
                 _____

Solar arc =   30   00 08

+ Natal MC   13 ♏ 02 15
                 _____

Prog MC =   43 ♏ 02 23 = 13 ♐ 02 23

116

MARY MOE

15 42 00 MDT =
21 42 00 GMT

PROGRESSIONS WORKSHEET 3

Progressed planetary positions for target date/time

* LEAP YEAR

Target date = Day # **325*** 21 42 00   Midnight date = Day #   **94**
Time   (GMT)   94   23 17 17   Time 23 17 17 (GMT)

Difference (n) =   230   22 24 43   (Decimalized = 230.93383)

	☉	☽
Position on later year day:	20 ♋ 23 16	12 ♑ 39 13
Position on earlier year day:	19 26 04	0 45 22
Travel:	57 12	11 53 51
[(Travel/365) x n] =	36 12	7 31 39
+ position on earlier day:	19 ♋ 26 04	0 ♑ 45 22
Position on target date=	20 ♋ 02 16	8 ♑ 17 01

	☿	♀	♂
Position on later year day:	16 ♌ 22.0	14 ♌ 42.2	7 ♎ 16.8
Position on earlier year day: (Reverse if ℞)	15 07.5	13 29.3	6 44.3
Travel:	1 14.5	1 12.9	32.5
[(Travel/365) x n} =	47.1	46.1	20.5
+ position on earlier day: (- if ℞)	15 ♌ 07.5	13 ♌ 29.3	6 ♎ 44.3
Position on target date =	15 ♌ 54.6	14 ♌ 15.4	7 ♎ 04.8

117

MARY MOE   **PROGRESSIONS WORKSHEET 4**   PROG. ☉
                                          ENTERS ♋

To find date/time progressed planet reaches target position

Midnight date = Day #   94   Time: 23 17 17 GMT

Target between midnight date _1975_ (earlier year) and _1976_ (later year)

Position on later day: 30 21 38   Target Position: 30 00 00

-Position on earlier day: 29 24 24   -Position on earlier day: 29 24 24

Travel (T1):   57 14   Travel (T2):   35 36

(If ℞, T1 = earlier-later, T2 = earlier-target)

[(T2 / T1) x 365] =   227 00 51 11   (Days/time)

+ midnight date/time: 94 23 17 17 GMT

Target date/time =   322 00 08 28 GMT = NOVEMBER 18, 1975

To find date of progressed lunation

Date of lunation: JULY 13 Day #   Degree of lunation: 21 ♑ 04
Time of lunation 17 01   (GMT)
Midnight date = Day #   Time:

Target between midnight date _1997_ (earlier year) and _1998_ (later year)

(Time of lunation / 24) x 365 = 258 19 05 00   (Days/time)

+ midnight date/time: 94 23 17 17

Date/time of prog. lunation = 353 18 22 17 = DECEMBER 19, 1997

118

MARY MOE   **PROGRESSIONS WORKSHEET 4** *PROG. ☽ ☌ NATAL Asc*
                                                      FOR SECOND TIME

To find date/time progressed planet reaches target position

Midnight date = Day #   94   Time: 23 17 17 GMT

Target between midnight date *1997* (earlier year) and *1998* (later year)

Position on later day: 24 30 28   Target Position: 19 ♑ 18 26

-Position on earlier day: 12 39 13   -Position on earlier day: 12   39   13

Travel (T1):   11 51 15   Travel (T2):   6   39 13

(If B, T1 = earlier-later, T2 = earlier-target)

[(T2 / T1) x 365] =   204   20 53 34   (Days/time)

+ midnight date/time: 94   23 17 17 GMT

Target date/time =   299   20 10 51 = OCTOBER 26, 1997

To find date of progressed lunation

Date of lunation: Day #   Degree of lunation:
Time of lunation   (GMT)
Midnight date = Day #   Time:

Target between midnight date _____(earlier year) and _____ (later year)

(Time of lunation / 24) x 365 =   (Days/time)

+ midnight date/time:
                        _____

Date/time of prog. lunation =

MARY MOE

Progressed MC = 13 ♐ 02 23 *Southern hemisphere, reverse* =
Closest MCs in table houses to prog MC = earlier: 12 ♐ 28   later: 13 ♐ 24
Distance earlier - later =   56   mins. (D1)
Distance earlier- prog MC = 34 23 mins. (D2)

Using lower latitude:
Asc for later sidereal time: 30 ♒ 41

Asc for earlier sidereal time: 29   10

Distance in mins. (D3) =   ___1___ ___31___

(D2 / D1) x D3 =   (D4)   55.87291

Asc for earlier sidereal time:
+ D4   29 ♒ 10

Unadjusted Asc =   30 ♒ 05.87291

Using earlier sidereal time:
Asc at higher lat: 28 ♒ 37
Asc at lower lat: 29 ♒ 10

Distance in mins =   33
x latitude factor
(mins of lat/60) =   (latitude correction)
   24.39228

Unadjusted Asc: 30 ♒ 05.87291

+/- Lat corr:
(if higher is higher, add) —   24.39228

Prog Asc =   *(Southern hemisphere, reverse)*

29 ♒ 41.48063

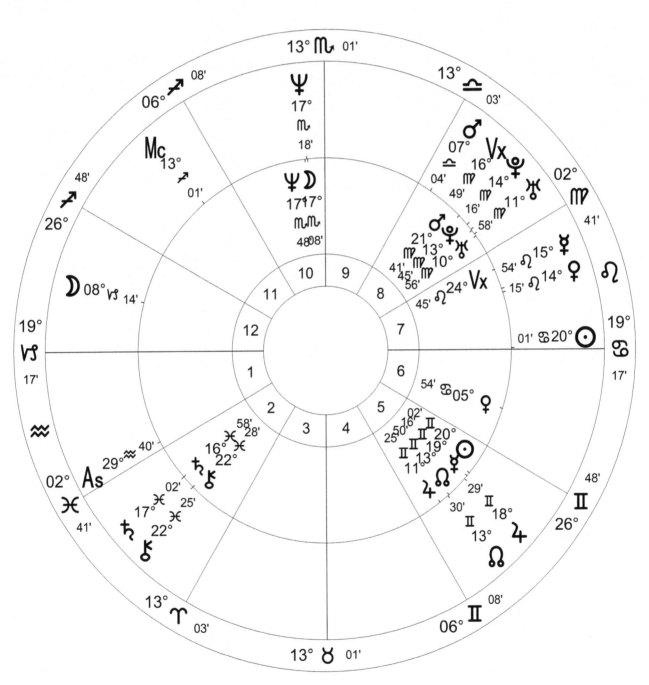

Inner Wheel
Mary Moe
Natal Chart
Jun 10 1965, Thu
10:25 pm MDT +6:00
Denver, CO
39°N44'21" 104°W59'03"
Geocentric
Tropical
Placidus
True Node

Outer Wheel
Mary Moe
Sec.Prog. SA in Long
Nov 19 1996, Tue
2:20 pm MDT +6:00
Denver, CO
39°N44'21" 104°W59'03"
Geocentric
Tropical
Placidus
True Node

PROGRESSIONS WORKSHEET 1

Name: WONG DOE

Date and Time of Birth (at Greenwich): SEPTEMBER 30, 1986   17 35 00 GMT

Midnight Date Calculation

Sidereal time at midnight Greenwich
for *Greenwich* birth date: 00   33   47

- Birth time (GMT):   -   17   35   00
                                                  —————————————
                                                  06   58   47

+ acceleration of birth time:
(10 secs/hour, 1 sec/6 mins.):   +   02   56
                                                  —————————————
Sidereal time for birth (STB) =   07   01   43

Midnight date = closest earlier ST = JAN. 6/7 (Same) previous year?

Time:
   ST later day: 07 05 03   STB: 07 01 43

   - ST earlier day: 07 01 07   - ST earlier day: 07 01 07
                    ——————————   ——————————
                     3 56 (ST1)   0 36 (ST2)

Time = [(ST2 / ST1) x 24] + midnight, earlier date = JANUARY 6, 1986 = DAY 6
                                                       03 39 40 GMT

123

WONG DOE   **PROGRESSIONS WORKSHEET 2**

Correlation of years with dates
(Greenwich birth date = year in which midnight date falls, then 1 day = 1 year)

Date	=	Year	Date	=	Year	Date	=	Year

(1986)

SEP 30 = 1986

OCT 5 = 1991

OCT 10 = 1996

OCT 15 = 2001

Calculation of progressed MC   APRIL 20, 1997

11 37 00 GMT

Progressed Sun: 17 ♎ 39   57

- Natal Sun: 07 ♎ 15   33

Solar arc =   10   24   24

+ Natal MC   1 ♉ 29   00

Prog MC =   11 ♉ 53   24

WONG DOE

APRIL 20, 1997   11 37 00 GMT

PROGRESSIONS WORKSHEET 3

Progressed planetary positions for target date/time

Target date = Day # 110 11 37 00   Midnight date = Day # 6
Time 11 37 00 (GMT)   6 03 39 40   Time 03 39 40 (GMT)

Difference (n) = 104 07 57 20   (Decimalized = 104.33148)

	☉	☽
Position on later year day:	18 ♎ 22 20	37 ♑ 06 39
Position on earlier year day:	17 23 00	23 08 07
Travel:	59 20	13 58 32
[(Travel/365) x n] =	16 57	3 59 41
+ position on earlier day:	+ 17 ♎ 23 00	+ 23 ♑ 08 07
Position on target date=	17 ♎ 39 57	27 ♑ 07 48

	☿	♀	♂
Position on later year day:	10 ♉ 57.8	20 ♉ 08.0	1 ♒ 38.2
Position on earlier year day: (Reverse if ℞)	9 39.3	19 58.5	1 04.7
Travel:	1 18.5	09.5	33.5
[(Travel/365) x n} =	22.4	02.7	09.5
+ position on earlier day: (- if ℞)	+ 9 ♉ 39.3	+ 19 ♉ 58.5	+ 1 ♒ 04.7
Position on target date =	10 ♉ 01.7	20 ♉ 01.2	1 ♒ 14.2

125

WONG DOE   **PROGRESSIONS WORKSHEET 4**   *PROG. ☽ ♂ NATAL IC*
FOR FIRST TIME

To find date/time progressed planet reaches target position

Midnight date = Day # 6   Time: 03 39 40 GMT

Target between midnight date _1991_ (earlier year) and _1992_ (later year)

Position on later day: 41 32 52   Target Position: 31 ♎ 29 00

-Position on earlier day: 27 17 15   -Position on earlier day: 27   17   15

Travel (T1):   14 15 37   Travel (T2):   04   11   45

(If B, T1 = earlier-later, T2 = earlier-target)

[(T2 / T1) x 365) =   107   09   28   33   (Days/time)

+ midnight date/time: 06   03   39   40   GMT

Target date/time =   113   13   08   13   =   APRIL 13, 1991

To find date of progressed lunation

Date of lunation: Day #   Degree of lunation:
Time of lunation   (GMT)
Midnight date = Day #   Time:

Target between midnight date _____ (earlier year) and _____ (later year)

(Time of lunation / 24) x 365 =   (Days/time)

+ midnight date/time:

Date/time of prog. lunation =

WONG DOE   **PROGRESSIONS WORKSHEET 4**   *PROG. ♂ ENTERS ≈*

To find date/time progressed planet reaches target position

Midnight date = Day #   6   Time: 03 39 40 GMT

Target between midnight date *1995* (earlier year) and *1996* (later year)

Position on later day: 30   31.5   Target Position: 30   00.0

-Position on earlier day: 29   58.6   -Position on earlier day: 29   58.6

Travel (T1):   32.9   Travel (T2):   1.4

(If в, T1 = earlier-later, T2 = earlier-target)

[(T2 / T1) x 365) =   15   12 45 58   (Days/time)

+ midnight date/time: 6   03 39 40 GMT

Target date/time =   21   16 25 38   = JANUARY 21, 1995

To find date of progressed lunation

Date of lunation: Day #   Degree of lunation:
Time of lunation   (GMT)
Midnight date = Day #   Time:

Target between midnight date _____(earlier year) and _____ (later year)

(Time of lunation / 24) x 365 =   (Days/time)

+ midnight date/time:

Date/time of prog. lunation =

WONG DOE

APRIL 20, 1997   11 37 00 GMT

PROGRESSIONS WORKSHEET 5
Calculation of progressed Asc   LF = 0.91666

Progressed MC = 11 ♉ 53 24 *Southern hemisphere, reverse =*
Closest MCs in table houses to prog MC = earlier: 11 ♉ 26   later: 12 ♉ 27
Distance earlier - later =   61 mins. (D1)
Distance earlier- prog MC =   27 24 mins. (D2)

Using lower latitude:
Asc for later sidereal time: 19 ♌ 58

Asc for earlier sidereal time: 19 ♌ 11

Distance in mins. (D3) =   47

(D2 / D1) x D3 =   (D4)   21.11147

Asc for earlier sidereal time: + 19 ♌ 11
+ D4

Unadjusted Asc =   19 ♌ 32.11147

Using earlier sidereal time:
Asc at higher lat: 19 ♌ 32
Asc at lower lat: 19 ♌ 11

Distance in mins =   21
x latitude factor
(mins of lat/60) =   19.24986   (latitude correction)

Unadjusted Asc: 19 ♌ 32.11147

+/- Lat corr:
 (if higher is higher, add) +   19.24986

Prog Asc =   19 ♌ 51.36133   *(Southern hemisphere, reverse)*

128

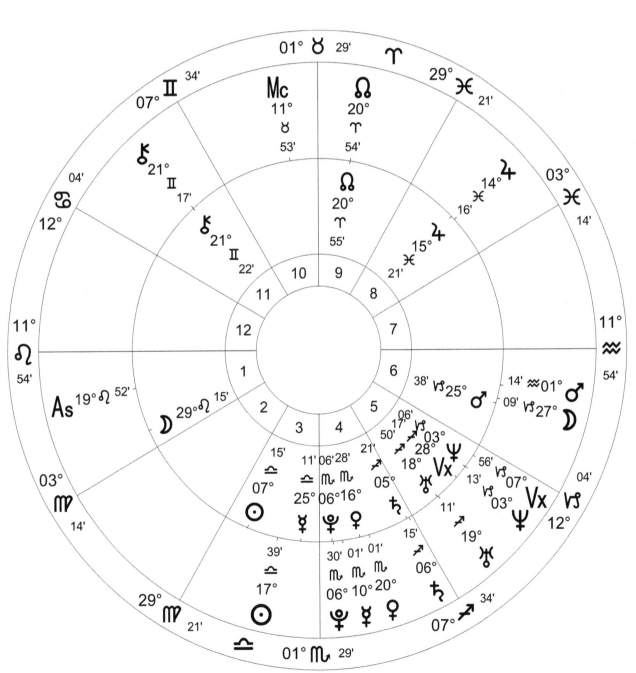

PROGRESSIONS WORKSHEET 1

Name: *KANGA ROE*

Date and Time of Birth (at Greenwich): *APRIL 6, 1975   13 32 00 GMT*

Midnight Date Calculation

Sidereal time at midnight Greenwich for *Greenwich* birth date:	12	54	39
- Birth time (GMT):	13	32	00
	23	22	39
+ acceleration of birth time: (10 secs/hour, 1 sec/6 mins.):		2	15
Sidereal time for birth (STB) =	23	24	54

Midnight date = closest earlier ST = *SEP 12/13* Same /(previous) year?

Time:

ST later day:	23 26 25		STB:		23 24 54	
- ST earlier day:	23 22 29		- ST earlier day:		23 22 29	
	3 56 (ST1)				2 25 (ST2)	

Time = [(ST2 / ST1) x 24] + midnight, earlier date = *SEPTEMBER 12, 1974 = DAY 255*

14 44 45 GMT

131

KANGA ROE   **PROGRESSIONS WORKSHEET 2**

Correlation of years with dates
(Greenwich birth date = year in which midnight date falls, then 1 day = 1 year)

Date	=	Year		Date	=	Year		Date	=	Year

(1975)

APRIL 6 = 1974

APRIL 11 = 1979

APRIL 16 = 1984

APRIL 21 = 1989

APRIL 26 = 1994

MAY 1 = 1999

Calculation of progressed MC   AUGUST 18, 1995

09 22 00 GMT

Progressed Sun:	36 ♈	03	32
- Natal Sun:	16 ♈	07	42
Solar arc =	19	55	50
+ Natal MC	9 ♎	11	43
Prog MC =	29 ♎	07	33

132

KANGA ROE

AUGUST 18, 1995   19 22 00 AEST =

PROGRESSIONS WORKSHEET 3   09 22 00 GMT

Progressed planetary positions for target date/time

Target date = Day # *230* 09 22 00   Midnight date = Day # *255*

Time *09 22 00*(GMT)   255 14 44 45   Time *14 44 45*(GMT)

Difference (n) =   25 05 22 45   (Decimalized = *340.22413*)

(*365 - 25*) = *340 05 22 45*   ☉   ☽

Position on later year day: 6 ♉ 07 30   21 ♏ 40 28

Position on earlier year day: 5   09 07   07   26 27

Travel: 58 23   14   14 01

[(Travel/365) x n] =   54 25   13   16 03

+ position on earlier day: + 5♉ 09 07   + 07 ♏ 26 27

Position on target date=   6♉ 03 32   20 ♏ 42 30

                                  ☿   ♀   ♂

Position on later year day: 15♉ 25.2   15♊ 17.8   11 ♓ 34.2

Position on earlier year day: 13   19.9   14   08.2   10   48.6
(Reverse if ℞)

Travel: 2   5.3   1   9.6   45.6

[(Travel/365) x n} =   1   56.8   1   04.9   42.5

+ position on earlier day: +13♉ 19.9   +14 ♊ 08.2   + 10♓ 48.6
(- if ℞)

Position on target date =   15♉ 16.7   15 ♊ 13.1   11 ♓ 31.1

KANGA ROE   **PROGRESSIONS WORKSHEET 4**   PROG. ⊙ ENTERS ♉

To find date/time progressed planet reaches target position

Midnight date = Day # 255   Time: 14 44 45 GMT

Target between midnight date 1988 (earlier year) and 1989 (later year)

Position on later day: 30 16 47   Target Position: 30 00 00

-Position on earlier day: 29 18 13   -Position on earlier day: 29 18 13
                         ————————   ————————
Travel (T1):   58 34   Travel (T2):   41 47

(If ℞, T1 = earlier-later, T2 = earlier-target)

[(T2 / T1) x 365) =   260   09 39 54   (Days/time)

+ midnight date/time: 255   14 44 45 GMT
                     ————————————————————
Target date/time =   516   00 24 39 GMT
                     -365
                     ————————
                      151   00 24 39 = MAY 31, 1989
                          To find date of progressed lunation
                                        PROG. FULL ☽ IN ♏

Date of lunation: APRIL 25 Day #   Degree of lunation: 4 ♏ 59
Time of lunation 19 55   (GMT)
Midnight date = Day # 255 Time: 14 44 45 GMT

Target between midnight date 1993 (earlier year) and 1994 (later year)

(Time of lunation / 24) x 365 = 302   21 35 00   (Days/time)

+ midnight date/time: 255   14 44 45 GMT
                              ————————————————————
Date/time of prog. lunation = 558   12 19 45
                              -365
                              ————————
                               193   12 19 45 GMT = JULY 12, 1994
       Murphy & Koch, The Math of Chart Construction (AFA)

KANGA ROE   **PROGRESSIONS WORKSHEET 4**   *PROG. D ENTERS ♋*
FOR FIRST TIME

To find date/time progressed planet reaches target position

Midnight date = Day # **255**   Time: **14 44 45 GMT**

Target between midnight date **1985** (earlier year) and **1986** (later year)

Position on later day: **42 04 38**   Target Position: **30 00 00**

-Position on earlier day: **28 38 29**   -Position on earlier day: **28 38 29**

Travel (T1): **13 26 09**   Travel (T2): **1 21 31**
          .43583

(If B, T1 = earlier-later, T2 = earlier-target)

[(T2 / T1) x 365) = **36 21 47 53** (Days/time)

+ midnight date/time: **255 14 44 45 GMT**

Target date/time = **292 12 32 38 GMT = OCTOBER 19, 1985**

To find date of progressed lunation

Date of lunation: Day #   Degree of lunation:
Time of lunation   (GMT)
Midnight date = Day #   Time:

Target between midnight date _____(earlier year) and _____ (later year)

(Time of lunation / 24) x 365 =   (Days/time)

+ midnight date/time:

Date/time of prog. lunation =

KANGA ROE   AUGUST 18, 1995   09 22 00 GMT

PROGRESSIONS WORKSHEET 5   LF = 0.86666

Calculation of progressed Asc

LATS 33/34 S

Progressed MC = 29≏01 33 *Southern hemisphere, reverse* = 29 ♈ 01 33

Closest MCs in table houses to prog MC = earlier: 29 ♈ 03   later: 0 ♉ 06

Distance earlier - later =   63   mins. (D1)

Distance earlier - prog MC = 4 30 mins. (D2)

Using lower latitude:

Asc for later sidereal time: 7 ♌ 58

Asc for earlier sidereal time: 7 ♌ 09

Distance in mins. (D3) =   49

(D2 / D1) x D3 =   (D4)   3.5

Asc for earlier sidereal time: 7 ♌ 09

+ D4   3.5

Unadjusted Asc =   7 ♌ 12.5

Using earlier sidereal time:

Asc at higher lat: 7 ♌ 33

Asc at lower lat: 7 ♌ 09

Distance in mins =   24

x latitude factor

(mins of lat/60) =   20.79984   (latitude correction)

Unadjusted Asc: 7 ♌ 12.5

+/- Lat corr: 20.79984

 (if higher is higher, add)

Prog Asc =   7♌ 33.29984   *(Southern hemisphere, reverse)* 7 ♒ 33.29984

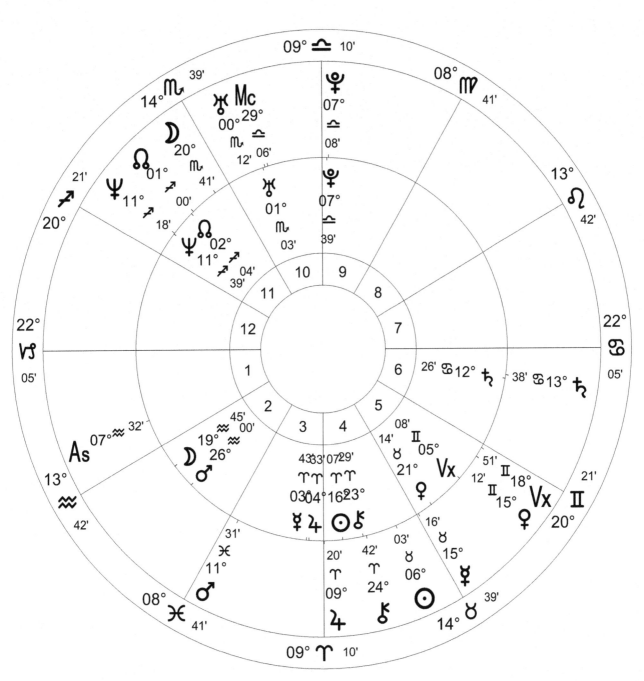

Chapter 14

Interpreting Progressed Charts

Progressed Cycles: A Subtle Prompt

Chapter 10 describes the more popular forms of progression used by astrologers today: secondary progressions and solar arc directions. In this chapter, we will be discussing the fundamental starting points for the interpretation of secondary progressions. We are discussing secondary progressions because they are the progressions most often used in describing the unfoldment of individual personality, and charting cycles of personal development.

Many astrologers working mainly with the timing of events prefer to use solar arc progressions, although these can certainly be used in interpretive work with individual charts as well. But, according to the experience of many astrologers, solar arc directions do seem to correspond to a more event-related sort of timing. For understanding individual personality and personal growth, secondary progressions seem to do an excellent job of illuminating some of the more subtle trends of individual development. Before we look at any specific kinds of progressions, it is important to reiterate a word of advice you have probably heard many times before in your study of astrological interpretation. Progressions can only be interpreted within the context of the natal chart. Just as transits cannot be fully understood unless understood within the context of the birth chart under consideration, neither can progressions be picked away and carried off individually, removed from the chart as a whole, if they are to be properly understood.

Progressions describe states of mind and mood, processes of personal unfoldment, "tones," and new experiences, both inner (in your emotional and psychological life) and outer (in the events of your life). Many of these cycles and tones are very personal and may be very subtle. Many will never show on the surface of an individual's life (through events) or in her everyday demeanor. Significant conjunctions, squares and oppositions formed by the transits of Jupiter, Saturn, Uranus, Neptune or Pluto to personal planets or angles in the chart almost always correspond to times during which there are events in a person's life, usually accompanied by various sorts of personal emotional, psychological, creative, spiritual, educational, or other kinds of learning experience, tumult, and transformation. Significant transits usually relate to cycles which are not subtle. Most transits are hard to overlook.

The cycles represented by progressions, especially secondary progressions, are easy to overlook. There is so much going on in anybody's life. If no big event comes down to hit you over the head, you may be more than happy to let a progressed cycle pass by unnoticed. Inner restlessness, yearnings and moods can often be ignored, or actually go unnoticed by many of us. So, it is quite possible that you, and many of your friends and clients, may not relate to every progressed aspect you see in a chart at a given time.

How reflective, self-aware and sensitive you are at any given time in your life will often determine how much you identify with a progression. Qualities like self-awareness and sensitivity are often spoke of as if they are carved in stone. "He is very self-aware," "She is very sensitive." But even the most self-aware person has periods in his life when he is wearing blinders, or when other needs and activities cloud his self-awareness. Even a sensitive person has times during which she can be insensitive, out of touch with what someone else is feeling, or unable to understand her own emotions and perceptions. Qualities like reflectiveness, self-awareness, and sensitivity fluctuate at various points in your life. At times, you will probably feel more perceptive and sensitive regarding the cycles represented by progressions than you will at others.

Another important consideration to note is that, if you are experiencing a lot of "transit action" at a given time (meaning you have one, two, three or more major transits livening up your chart) it may be easy to overlook, or simply not really feel the energy of a symbolic progressed cycle.

If either of these scenarios is true for you or a client, i.e. (1) you are not feeling very reflective, self-aware, or sensitive due to ill health, stress, depression or a busy everyday life, or (2) you are so caught up in other activities, inner processes or "vibes" that you are not relating well to the potentials an important secondary progression may represent for you, take the time to simply illuminate the possible potentials of the progression in a clear way.

Consider the interpretation of the progression in a clear, simple way. For example, progressed Sun conjunct natal Mars opens the potential for asserting yourself in a new way, for experiencing your sexual energy in a new way, for growing in confidence. Even if you do not feel any of those things going on right now, or even if you feel the opposite is true, keep the potentials clear in your mind. These are subtle, often deeply interior energies. Sometimes, consciously opening the door to them is one of the best ways to invite them surface in more powerful ways.

Never expect that you will learn more from studying progressions than from studying transits. This does not seem to be the case. Transits are an amazingly enlightening tool. The cycles reflected by the symbolism of transits are vital, often attention-getting, and provide a complex, yet integrative look at the ongoing unfoldment of an individual's life and personal development. Transits must never be abandoned in favor of progressions alone. Transits can, in fact, provide so much "meaty" information regarding the cycle of an individual's life and personal development, that you may question why progressions might be anything more than an entertaining interpretive novelty, or an antiquated predictive tool.

But we would never call progressions a novelty, or advocate abandoning progressions in favor of transits alone. The mere fact that a cycle is quieter, and expresses more in an internal way, does not make it any less meaningful. The fact that it may require a little work to see and feel a tone, feeling, mood, urge or potential within, or to see or create an opportunity for something new and personally meaningful, does not make a cycle less powerful. Transits can be flashy and attention-getting. Progressions are likely to be subtle and quietly persistent. Important sometimes in terms of events, but most likely to be meaningful if we instinctively or consciously work to bring out the potentials they point toward, like cosmic background music, urging that "the time is right for . . ."

What progressions are important?

Astrologers have many different answers to this question. We will address progressions of the Sun in aspect to natal planets and angles, and sign changes of the progressed Sun. We will also address lunar progressions, including the progression of the Moon through the houses, which seems to be especially significant in interpretation, and which tends to result in more noticeable shifts than most progressed events. The progressions of the Sun and Moon seem to have the most consistent, observable interpretative significations. There are other progressed events worth noting, and these will be discussed also. But, as we said earlier, no progression can be properly understood outside the context of the natal chart. Progressions and transits work only in relation to the natal chart. They bring out potentials which already exist in the natal chart. They show us the timing that each individual will experience in working through various issues, and harnessing energies, feelings, and urges in various new ways, but only as indicated in the natal chart.

As with all astrological symbols, interpretation must be done in close alliance with the individual for whom the chart has been drawn. This is especially true for progressions, because of their often interior, intimate nature. The best astrological interpretation will be made by considering the whole person. Interpretation in the abstract, such as that which we offer here for educational purposes, can never be as in-depth as the true application of the art of astrology to an actual human being. What is offered in this chapter are guidelines, loose-fitting rules, keywords to stimulate your perceptions.

The Progressed Sun

Progressions of the Sun to natal planets by conjunction, square or opposition indicate times during which the nature of the natal planet will be emphasized. We recommend the use of a very tight orb for determining progressed aspects, no more than thirty minutes to one degree, maximum. An appropriate orb of time for the anticipated duration of a progressed solar cycle may be from about six months to one year surrounding the exact aspect.

The conjunction is the most powerful of these aspects. Its duration may extend for a full year, and its "effects" may be experienced with more immediacy and intensity than other solar progressions. Conjunctions of the progressed Sun to natal planets, or the natal Ascendant or MC (or to progressed planets or the progressed Ascendant or MC) are usually less subtle than other progressed cycles.

In addition to the major challenging aspects, we recommend noting the semisextile aspects of the progressed Sun to natal planets, again using a tight orb, which may be effective for up to six months surrounding the exact aspect.

What might be expected when the progressed Sun forms an aspect with a natal planet?

1. The drive represented by the natal planet may be emphasized, agitated, excited, in a subtle, but intense way.

2. Realizations about the symbolism of the natal planet may come to light during this period, especially if one opens the door to such insights by being conscious of new possibilities.

3. Restlessness, anger or frustration may be activated in the context of the expression of the drive represented by the natal planet.

4. There may be feelings of embarrassment, humiliation, or disappointment with respect to some way in which you are expressing the drive represented by the natal planet, or some way in which you have expressed it in the past.

If you do find youself experiencing these kinds of feelings, or the angry, frustrated feelings mentioned above, remember that these kinds of emotional reactions often color the onset of a progressed cycle and usually seem geared toward opening your eyes toward some way in which change is required. It is through finding ways to deal with, express, overcome and otherwise respond to these kinds of churning inner emotions that progressions of the Sun to natal planets often become times of meaningful personal growth.

All progressions of the Sun to natal planets, the Ascendant or the MC can be excellent times to initiate a change of outgrown modes of self-expression. All progressions of the Sun represent times during which you may be ready for personal change, for transformation of your sense of identity, self-image, and in terms of the role(s) you are playing in life. This process of change often involves recognition of the need for self-awareness, and for some conscious level of self-initiated change. Otherwise, these cycles can be times of intense feelings of dissatisfaction, restlessness, and aimlessness, or misdirected sensations of excessive pride or egotism.

Let's look at some of the keywords that can help you in making interpretations of the progressed Sun's aspects to the natal planets. We will use the convention of writing P/ before a planet to indicate a reference to a progressed planet, and N/ to indicate a reference to a natal planet.

P/Sun in Aspect to N/Sun

This is obviously a limited subject. The first major aspect would be a sextile, which would occur at about age 60, and the next a square at about age 90. However, the semisextile at about age 30, and the semisquare at about age 45 may be very significant.

Emphasized sense of self. Self-realization. There may be restlessness, anger and frustration directed to yourself, possible embarrassment or disppointment, or enlightenment as to past or present circumstances or self-expression, which can result in cycles of subtle or radical personal change.

<%-2>This can be a time of enhanced self-confidence, self-esteem and self-knowledge, a time for feeling accepted and lovable. These feelings may arise on their own, or through affirming and nurturing circumstances or relationships. Sometimes, these changes emerge within the context of some challenging or disruptive emotional events or life circumstances. Often, as is so typically the case in life, it is a mixture of both.

P/Sun in Aspect to N/Moon

Emphasized sense of mood. Emotional realizations. There may be emotional restlessness, anger or frustration, possible embarrassment, disappointment or enlightenment about past or present circumstances, or emotional attachments, attitudes, needs or habits. This may result in cycles of subtle or radical emotional change.

P/Sun in Aspect to N/Mercury

Emphasized sense of mind. Logical realizations about your own goals, educational aspirations, intellectual abilities, or style of communication.

There may be restlessness, dissatisfaction or disillusionment affecting these areas of life, which may result in subtle or radical change in attitudes, opinions, ideas, habits, or methods or style of communication. This will be true especially if there are major transits going on when the progressed aspect is exact.

P/Sun in Aspect to N/Venus

<%-2>Emphasized sense of relationship and yearning. Realizations about love, money, and your sense of values. There is usually less overt restlessness here, and more of an urge towards establishing or accepting harmony in some new way.

There can be a sense of disillusionment or enlightenment regarding past or present needs, attitudes or personal behavior in a significant relationship. This may result in abandonment of an outgrown pattern or habit in favor of something new. Sometimes, there are distinct changes in your love life, a marriage, a break-up, meeting someone new. Such overt results are more likely if major transits are occurring when the progressed aspect is exact.

P/Sun in Aspect to N/Mars

Emphasized sense of assertiveness. Realizations regarding self-image, sense of direction, or sexuality. There may well be a heightening of physical or emotional restlessness, or anger, a sense of embarrassment, disappointment or frustration regarding past or present actions, attitudes, or circumstances.

There may well be a rejuvenated sense of confidence or self-knowledge, which may result in a cycle of shedding outgrown ways in favor of more personally exciting, challenging goals and behavior patterns. A personal sexual revolution may be initiated during this cycle. Again, the presence of major transits coinciding with the exact progressed aspect may be significant in fostering external events.

P/Sun in Aspect to N/Jupiter

Emphasized feeling of "possibility". Realizations about opportunity, success, personal growth, happiness. Enhanced feelings of optimism. Restlessness can be greatly exaggerated. There may be a rejuvenated sense of confidence or self-knowledge. A time when restraints can be dropped, and when outgrown limitations, self-definitions, or definitions placed on one by family, society, or a culture, can be dispensed with or transcended.

New opportunities, experiences and interests are very possible during these cycles, especially the conjunction. This most often seems to be the case because during virtually all cycles involving Jupiter, there is a sense of being drawn toward the future in some significant way, and the sensation of an inner-generated desire or demand for happiness, or a new definition of success in one's life. "Settling for" something, or "just getting by", in just about any situation, does not go over very well during most Jupiter cycles, including solar progressed aspects to Jupiter. There is often some kind of inner prompting, which urges you almost irresistably towards making changes, and striving for happiness, "breaking free", or expanding horizons.

P/Sun in Aspect to N/Saturn

Emphasized sense of security. Realizations about security or insecurity, goals, fears, authority, definition, feelings of restriction. There can be feelings of frustration, or of crystallization, organization or consolidation regarding present constraints, limitations or commitments. There may be feelings of embarrassment, disappointment, or frustration relating to past or present circumstances, relationships, or aspects of oneself, which can result in subtle or radical personal changes in one's life's framework, for example one's career, job, living arrangements, major relationships, or everyday schedule.

You may be drawn into an absorption of fears, insecurity, depression, negative thinking, or apparently chaotic situations, emotionally or in actual circumstances, often just prior to experiencing or initiating some major personal change. Again, this is most often true in conjunction with some major transit.

P/Sun in Aspect to N/Uranus

Emphasized sense of individuality, freedom, independence, rebellion. Possible creative realizations, and realizations concerning liberation, accompanied by feelings of physical restlessness. Feelings of embarrassment, disappointment, frustration or enlightenment regarding past or present circumstances may inspire some "sudden," spontaneous self-interested or self-motivated changes. You may also be drawn to selfishness, insensitivity, recklessness, or very single-minded behavior, often just prior to experiencing or initiating some major personal change.

P/Sun in Aspect to N/Neptune

Emphasized sense of faith. Possible spiritual or creative realizations, which may be liberating. Strong restlessness is possible on any and all levels. There may also be a sense of confusion, disappointment, and intense emotional experiences, which may inspire subtle or radical personal growth and change.

You may be drawn towards escapism, or self-deception, or experience a sense of dissolution or aimlessness in terms of your self-image, often just prior to experiencing or initiating some major personal change.

P/Sun in Aspect to N/Pluto

Emphasized sense of "letting go," surrendering to "fate." Realizations regarding one's past are possible. There may be considerable anger, frustration, or sense of loss. There may be subtle or radical power struggles, or breaks with the past, which can result in cycles of personal transformation, especially in conjunction with major transits operating at the time of the exact progressed aspect.

If there is any progressed solar aspect coming exact during this year in your chart, especially a conjunction, re-read the section on P/Sun in aspect with N/Sun. All progressions of the Sun involve the solar archetype. All these progressed cycles are likely to correspond with times during which many of the qualities traditionally associated with the Sun and Leo are likely to be major issues. Therefore, during any progression of the Sun to any natal planet, an issue of self-awareness is likely to be at the heart of any restlessness, or urge to change. All such progressions are also likely to relate to very personal cycles of change, often occurring within oneself, and one's own outlook and emotions. These changes may not ever be easily visible to others, and may sometimes be difficult to verbalize, although you may be able to perceive subtle shifts and changes within yourself.

During conjunctions or challenging aspects of the progressed Sun with natal planets or angles, your sense of self is likely to be emphasized in some new way. There can be many self-realizations, and change is likely to take on a very personal tone.

Progressed Sun Changing Sign or House

A change of sign by the progressed Sun is a major event, which occurs only at intervals of about thirty years. While the Sun's natal sign remains the most significant interpretive guide throughout one's life, the progression of the Sun into another sign adds an overlay of that sign. For example, a person born with the Sun in Aries will always have a self-assertive, individualistic, and perhaps aggressive personality, but when the progressed Sun enters Taurus, she will also have access to a more subtle layer of venusian values. This may result, for example, in settling down in a fixed abode for the first time, or developing a new appreciation for the aesthetic side of life, especially during the period of some consistent major transit.

It is also important to note any change of house by the progressed Sun, according to whatever house system you prefer to use. There are not many consistent interpretive guidelines to offer here, because the range of event experiences seems very wide, and because house changes do not always correspond to events, but more often signify subtle shifts in outlook, and emotional energies and orientations. But, by noting house changes, you are able to use your own powers of observation to perceive events involving personal change. These may correspond to the progressed cycle, and may offer insights, especially when considered with consistent major transits. Furthermore, the house position of the progressed Sun will suggest areas of life likely to be affected by sign changes, or aspects of the progressed Sun with natal planets or angles.

Solar Progressions to the Ascendant and MC Axes

As mentioned above, it is a good idea to keep note of progressions of the Sun by house. Interpret these progressions not only in light of the kind of aspect involved (i.e. sextile, square, etc.) to the natal Ascendant, but also in light of equal house interpretations. For example, a progression of the Sun thirty degrees from the Ascendant might correspond to a time during which there is a "tone" of the second house activated for the individual, lots of money issues, things stimulating analysis of her values and so on, her sense of grounding and connection to her environment. A progression of the Sun a hundred twenty degrees from the Ascendant might correspond to a time during which there is a fifth house "tone," according to the equal house cusp involved in the aspect. Equal house interpretations (because the progressions are activating equal house cusps) have a more personalized meaning deriving from their aspect relationship with the ascending degree. (See *Equal Houses* by Beth Koch, AFA, 1992). These points seem especially "sensitive" to the touch of the progressed Sun.

Any progression to the Ascendant (especially conjunction, square, and opposition) also activates the Descendant. The Ascendant is part of an axis. Any progression, or for that matter any transit or natal aspect, which stimulates the Ascendant, also stimulates the Descendant. Therefore, these cycles are likely to be related to times which are not only significant in terms of personal change, but which raise Descendant (interpersonal) issues as well.

The same holds true for any progressed aspect to the MC. This is an aspect to the MC-IC axis, and is likely to relate to a period of about six months to one year, during which career and home issues, and the striving for a sense of identity and role in the world may be in the spotlight in a subtle or radical way. Your issues around home, family, "roots," and security are likely to be emphasized.

Progressions of the Moon

The Moon moves relatively quickly compared to the other progressed astrological bodies. It virtually soars through the progressed chart. As it does so, its progressions mark a very subtle kind of emotional rhythm or unfoldment. It is difficult to interpret the progressed Moon in a consistent way from chart to chart. The Moon represents a very fundamental life orientation. In traditional astrology, this was called "temperament." What could be more fundamental or integral to personality than that?

Attempts at rigid definitions of lunar progressions are likely to fall short because of the highly personalized nature of the Moon. We will not attempt to provide universal definitions here. But, as in the case of the progressed Sun, changes of sign or house by the progressed Moon, and to a lesser extent, aspects of the progressed Moon to natal planets and angles, may result in subtle effects involving the expression of the planet or angle concerned. The conjunction of the progressed Moon to the natal Ascendant is significant in relation to the expression of one's personality. The return of the progressed Moon to its natal position can point towards the potential for a new beginning or emotional rebirth, especially under the influence of a significant transit. Progressed lunations (i.e. the progressed Sun conjunct or opposite the progressed Moon) are also very significant in ways analogous to the significance of a new Moon or full Moon birth in the natal chart. A progressed new Moon indicates the beginning of a new cycle of understanding or enlightenment. A progressed full Moon indicates the culmination of this understanding or enlightenment, and the beginning of a time to integrate it into one's life, and share it with the world. The sign and house in which a progressed lunation occurs offer further interpretive guidance.

You may notice twists and turns in your emotional life, related to a planet or point in the natal chart touched by the progressed Moon. The conjunction seems to be by far the most significant of the progressed lunar aspects, although the square and opposition are also worthy of note. Because the progressed Moon moves so quickly, these cycles are likely to be felt for about one month. Often, within that month span, an event or emotional experience or change in mood related to the symbolism of the planet touched by the progressed Moon occurs. There may also be a marked increase in restlessness and emotional energy, or memories from the past stimulated while a planet is touched by the progressed Moon.

The Progressed Moon Through the Houses

The progression of the Moon through all twelve signs, and through all twelve houses, takes about twenty-seven to twenty-eight years (a reminder of the Saturnian cycle). This means that it will take the progressed Moon about two and one half years to journey through a sign, or a thirty degree equal house. It will take a variable length of time to move through a Placidus or Koch house, depending on the size of the house in question.

It is interesting to note the time period during which the progressed Moon enters the sign of the natal Moon. It is especially important to note the time frame of several months surrounding its return to its exact natal degree. This is called a progressed lunar return, and can be a time during which there is clearly a sense of "new birth," or new beginning of some kind in your life, or on various emotional levels. As with any period of "new birth," this cycle may include some sense of loss, closure, reorganization, a break from the past, or some distinct sense of the ending of a chapter, as a prelude to the start of a new chapter. As the progressed Moon enters its natal sign, you may begin to feel this sense of closure more distinctly. This will be true especially if you are emotionally perceptive, artistic, sensitive or intuitive by nature. You may begin to feel changes in the air, long before there are perceptible changes in actual, tangible areas of your life. As the progressed Moon makes the conjunction with its natal degree, you may experience anticipation, and become aware of the ways in which you are entering a new emotional cycle, or a new cycle of personal development or identity.

Interpret the progressed lunar return in relation to the natal Moon. This is a cycle related to the growth or maturation of your emotional self, your self-expression, and your identity (sense of who you are). It will probably point toward new awarenesses, new expressions, the dropping of past inhibitions, limitations and baggage related to natal lunar aspects. So, look closely at the "lunar complex," all aspects involving the Moon in your natal chart, and consider the natal Moon sign, to get some insight into what is involved during this important lunar progression.

Virtually any progressions of the Moon through a natal house can relate to a sense of closure regarding the affairs of that house. For example, there may be a sense of closure regarding affairs of the twelfth house as the progressed Moon moves into the first house. As the progressed Moon changes houses, there may also be a sense of growing anticipation regarding the affairs of the house into which it will now journey. For example, as the Moon crosses the Ascendant and moves into the first house, there may be an increasing sense of anticipation and excitement in your personal life, your self-confidence, etc.

New awarenesses, a new sense of self-expression and intensity of moods and feelings related to the area and dimensions of experience symbolized by the house into which the progressed Moon is moving are also possibilities. Gradually, there may be a spotlight of focus on emotional issues related to that house and the realm of experience it represents, and, as the progressed Moon moves through the house over the course of about two and one half years, there may be a slow but steady process of coming to terms with these emotional issues, and a "letting go" of emotional baggage in this area.

As the progressed Moon conjuncts any house cusp, there may be a corresponding event related to the affairs of that house, or the dimension of experience related to that house, or an experience which stirs emotional issues related to the house in question.

Following are guidelines for interpreting the progression of the Moon through the houses.

Progressed Moon Conjunct Ascendant, in First House

As the progressed Moon conjoins the Ascendant, and moves into the early degrees of the first house, there can be a sense of closure of a time during which there may have been great shifts and swings in your emotions and moods. It may be a time of spiritual, creative, emotional and psychological searching, which may yield to a time during which you experience a growing urge to put new perceptions, ideals, insights and ideas into action. You may feel a refreshed sense of confidence, a new sense of self, and overall feelings of hopefulness and excitement. Your moods may be intense, even restless, but probably largely optimistic. Look to the natal rising sign and aspects for further insight here. For example, a Cancer or Pisces Ascendant may experience more complex or intense mood swings than an Aries or Sagittarius Ascendant.

Personal baggage of all kinds can be dropped during the period of months surrounding the progressed Moon's conjunction with the Ascendant, and as the progressed Moon journeys through the first house. This period can feel like a "new chapter." There is the chance to have a "clean slate" in some way, especially on emotional levels. Sensations of anticipation and a vibration of "new beginning" are likely to be strong.

During the several months surrounding the progressed Moon's exact conjunction with the Ascendant, there can be a key event in your personal life, or a significant emotional event.

Progressed Moon Conjunct Second House Cusp, in Second House

As the progressed Moon conjoins the second house cusp, and moves through the second house, there can be a sense of closure surrounding feelings of self-expansion, with a growing emphasis on establishing greater grounding or security in both emotional and practical terms. New ways of earning a living may occupy your attention. An emphasis on "acquisition" is possible. This may be expressed not only through the actual acquisition of possessions, but through strong yearnings for new friends, lifestyle changes, money, security, knowledge, or new experiences. There may be significant events relating to finances, possessions, or your sense of security.

Progressed Moon Conjunct Third House Cusp, in Third House

As the progressed Moon conjoins the cusp of the third house, and moves into the early degrees of the third house, a cycle of acquisition or "gathering" may gradually yield to an increasing urge toward distribution of knowledge, shared experience, communication, interaction, teaching, etc. There can be a growing sense of intellectual curiosity and stimulation during the passage of the progressed Moon through this house. In response to these interior promptings, you may adopt a new hobby, interest or passion. There may be a significant event relating to your education, your peers, or family (especially siblings) or one which stimulates your urge to communicate, write, travel, learn or teach.

Progressed Moon Conjunct Fourth House Cusp, in Fourth House

As the progressed Moon conjoins the fourth house cusp, and moves through the early degrees of the fourth house, you may feel the urge to reel in your energies, especially your emotional energies. A time of wider diversification of your intellectual and emotional energies may gradually yield to a time during which you feel the urge to focus in a more concentrated kind of way.

A sense of anticipation and excitement related to home, family matters, or your personal life can color the progressed Moon's journey through this house. A strong focus on emotional purging is possible during this time. This can also be a time during which you feel the weight of all sorts of emotional baggage. This may be true particularly during the earlier portion of the progressed Moon's journey. The increased intensity of emotional energies during this cycle may inspire you to take a closer look at your feelings, and, by the end of the progressed Moon's occupancy of the fourth house, you may find yourself coming to new terms with many of your emotions, or letting go of unnecessary baggage. The ease with which you let go of this kind of stuff may be proportional to the efforts which you make to do so, so it can be a terrific time to get involved in some kind of counselling, self-awareness work, astrology, art, or some other deliberate effort aimed at giving attention to your feelings.

During the several months surrounding the progressed Moon's exact conjunction with the IC, there can be a move, a family or an emotional event, or something involving dreams, or spiritual or psychic experience, which may prove inspiring or even catalytic in your personal life. Because the fourth house is an angular house, this leg of the progressed Moon's journey can be a time when the potential for a "new beginning" of some kind is strong.

Progressed Moon Conjunct Fifth House Cusp, in Fifth House

As the progressed Moon conjoins the fifth house cusp, and moves through the early degrees of the fifth house, there may be a sense of closure coming to a time during your life which might have been emotionally analytical or self-protective. Over the course of the progressed Moon's passage through this house, you may feel this vibration gradually yield to a time during which you are feeling more expressive emotionally and creative in new ways.

Affairs of the heart may feel lighter and more playful with the progressed Moon in this house. There may be a sense of excitement in your creative life or personal life. You may feel in the mood to take emotional or creative risks. You may feel increasingly liberated from emotional baggage of some kind, and your thirst for fun, adventure and self-expression of all kinds may grow in proportion to the lightening of your emotional load. There may even be an event which is pure fun (often in a memorable way) or an event involving your children, or which leads you to expand your boundaries (especially emotional boundaries) in some new direction.

Progressed Moon Conjunct Sixth House cusp, in Sixth House

During the progressed Moon's passage through the sixth house, there can be a gradual emergence of a new sense of direction in your life, especially in terms of work and practical affairs. There can also be a sense of growing excitement or satisfaction regarding your work, your everyday life, or whatever service you perform for others. There might be satisfaction with, or anxiety about, your health. You may be prompted to begin a new regimen of diet or exercise. Often, there are new developments in the everyday ins-and-outs of your working life, and these may affect your mood. Moods and feelings relating to your subjective sense of order and accomplishment may surface. During the several months surrounding the progressed Moon's exact conjunction with the sixth house cusp, there may be a significant event in the area of your work, health, security, responsibilities, or sense of service or obligation to others.

Progressed Moon Conjunct Seventh House Cusp, in Seventh House

As the progressed Moon conjoins the Descendant, and moves through the early degrees of the seventh house, there can be a sense of closure of a cycle of work and ground-laying. This vibration may yield, gradually or swiftly, to a more outward-moving phase, in which a sense of anticipation or excitement in relationship is possible. A new person, people, or idea(s) may be stimulating. This can be true in your love life, but it may equally be true in other important relationships, such as business partnerships, or other collaborations.

Baggage from past relationships can often be dropped during the progressed Moon's passage through the seventh house. Emotional baggage related to a present relationship can be worked through during this time. Sometimes, this may mean that a relationship comes to an end during this cycle. But there can also be new beginnings, either within an existing relationship, or in the form of the beginning of a new one. The potential for beginnings and endings extends generally to love, friendship, and any other kind of relationship.

During the several months surrounding the progressed Moon's exact conjunction with the cusp of the seventh house, there may be an important emotional event or development in your marriage, love life, or other important relationships. Because the seventh is an angular house, there may be a strong sense of "new beginning" coloring the time frame during which the progressed Moon journeys through this house.

Progressed Moon Conjunct Eighth House Cusp, in Eighth House

Beginnings or endings of relationships are also possible as the progressed Moon conjoins the eighth house cusp, and moves through the early degrees of the eighth house. This may be true especially in the case of sexual relationships, or relationships with intense emotional overtones. There may be an increased sense of excitement, anticipation, or even preoccupation with sex, taboo subjects and activities, money, career and power.

There can be a great deal of emotional baggage to work through during this cycle, with the possibility of many emotional issues surfacing and demanding attention. There can be a lot of battling with yourself and with others during the progressed Moon's passage through this house, which may either be a trigger for the necessary emotional work, or the catalyst for dealing with emotional issues. Much of the battling is likely to be in the areas of sex, money, career, ambition, and power.

There is likely to be an intensity surrounding your creative effort while the progressed Moon is in the eighth house. There will be an intensity in your efforts toward self-awareness, your ambitions, and your search for meaning. There can be a strong urge toward emotional purging during this time.

During the several months surrounding the progressed Moon's exact conjunction with the eighth house cusp, there may be an emotionally significant, potent, meaningful event in your life in some area symbolized by the eighth house.

Progressed Moon Conjunct Ninth House Cusp, in Ninth House

A phase of emotional intensity gradually yields to one of increased intellectual curiosity and the urge to communicate, as the progressed Moon conjoins the ninth house cusp, and moves through the early degrees of the ninth house. Learning may feel increasingly exciting, and may come easily, during this time.

The progressed Moon's passage through the ninth house is a time during which you may be feeling your aspirations in a new way. Future planning, dreaming, and the setting of long-term goals may all be on your mind. A renewed sense of faith, hope, and optimism may prevail, and you may be feeling increasingly philosophical or interested in the pursuit of knowledge, wisdom, and the active expression of your values, faith, or ideals.

During the several months surrounding the exact conjunction of the progressed Moon with the ninth house cusp, there may be travel or educational opportunities, or some inspiring or intellectually stimulating event.

Progressed Moon Conjunct Tenth House Cusp, in Tenth House

There can be the attainment of a goal early in this cycle, especially in the months surrounding the exact conjunction of the progressed Moon with the cusp of the tenth house. Attainment and accomplishment can highlight the entire period of the progressed Moon's occupancy of this house. A sense of excitement and anticipation may color your career and goals.

A new way of expressing yourself or seeing yourself may be possible. You may take on a new role in life. A restructuring of your career or personal life is possible. If you feel that you are "stuck" in a rut, playing a role which you are finding increasingly empty, you may feel yourself increasingly drawn toward doing something else which appeals to you on a gut level, or reflects the creative side of you. You may find youself shedding any roles in which you are just "going through the motions," updating your lifestyle and self-image in the process.

During the several months surrounding the progressed Moon's exact conjunction with the tenth house cusp, there can be a key event or development in your career, or a significant event influencing your self-image, or the way in which others view you. Because the tenth is an angular house, the potential for a distinct "new beginning" of some sort is very strong.

Progressed Moon Conjunct Eleventh House Cusp, in Eleventh House

As the progressed Moon conjoins the eleventh house cusp, and moves through the early degrees of the eleventh house, there can be a sense of closure of a cycle during which there may have been much change in your career. This may gradually yield to a time during which you are able to see the impact that recent events have produced, especially in the lives of others, and in terms of your own recognition among peers (in groups, clubs, organizations, your social circle, among friends, etc.). There may be a sense of excitement in your public life and in opportunities for relating to others. Your moods may fluctuate in relation to your sense of friendship, and contribution to those around you. There may be a gradual feeling of liberation in your self-expression, in expression of your ideas and opinions.

During the several months surrounding the progressed Moon's exact conjunction with the eleventh house cusp, there can be an event which relates to your growing sense of community involvement or future aspirations.

Progressed Moon Conjunct Twelfth House Cusp, in Twelfth House

The progressed Moon's conjunction with this cusp and journey through the twelfth house can mark a very emotional period. There may be great intensity to your moods during this time. Emotional, creative and psychological energies may be intensified. Also, intuition may be heightened, and spiritual inclinations stirred. A restless, aimless vibration may create a background vibration within you as you grapple with all kinds of emotions.

But there is the potential to drop baggage of all kinds during this cycle. You can transcend, come to new terms, find enlightenment, and have all manner of emotional experiences. Often these come only after a period of disillusionment, confusion, and soul-searching. You may see the world through rose-colored glasses during this time (usually early in the cycle) but this tendency may change suddenly as the progressed Moon makes her way through the twelfth house, thereby opening you up to the experience of seeing things in a completely new light. During the several months surrounding the progressed Moon's exact conjunction with the twelfth house cusp, there may be a key spiritual or emotional event of some kind.

Other Significant Progressions

Other significant progressed cycles should also be noted. The following represent some of the progresions we believe are worthy of special note.

Progressed Ascendant and MC

Note any change in the progressed rising sign. This can relate to a significant sense of personal liberation, shift or expansion in one's vision of life and sense of self. According to the nature of the signs involved, there can be a sense of new doors opening, of a new perspective. On a subtle, interior level, feelings of anticipation, renewed enthusiasm, and feelings of "new possibility" may emerge. A change in the progressed rising sign can mark a year of dramatic, significant shifts in consciousness or outlook, especially if supported by a major transit. There is potentially transformative energy here, a possible new beginning or new vision of yourself.

The same holds true for progressions of the sign on the MC, although the shifts in consciousness involved here may be even more subtle than those represented by progressions to the Ascendant. Remember, progressions are more likely to form background themes of emotional restlessness, or subtle change and growth within. There may or may not be actual changes in your career, identity or role in life during the period of about six months to one year surrounding a change in the progressed MC sign, but the potential for this is certainly heightened at this time.

Planetary Sign Changes

Any change of sign by a progressed planet may have significance, and should be noted. There may not be actual changes related to the nature of the planet and sign involved, but the potential is there. Undoubtedly, there will be an internal evolution of the function of the planet concerned. For example, a change of sign by progressed Mercury from Cancer to Leo may signal increased confidence or brashness in communication and self-expression, a greater willingness to say what one thinks. A change of sign of progressed Venus from Libra to Scorpio may suggest an internal shift away from compromise in relationship and towards greater self-protective calculation. Whether any of these trends will be expressed in terms of actual events may depend on transits or other life events. Sign changes are especially significant in the case of the outer planets, because they are rare events. Often, a progressed outer planet will not change sign during a lifetime, and, if it does, it will do so only once. When such a change occurs, it usually marks a major shift in the energy represented by that planet, and will not pass unnoticed.

Changes in Progressed Planetary Motion

The year during which any progressed planet changes its motion from direct to retrograde, or retrograde to direct, may be a time during which there are shifts and changes in an individual's consciousness, feelings, identity and outlook in relation to the drive represented by the planet in question.

When a planet stations and turns retrograde, the energy represented by that planet frequently becomes internalized and intensified, and its outward expression often becomes correspondingly more difficult, eccentric and unpredictable. Instead of supporting other planetary energies, it may appear to "go its own way." (For an excellent detailed analysis of this process, we strongly recommend *Retrograde Planets: Traversing the Inner Landscape* by Erin Sullivan, Arkana, 1992.) When this occurs by progression, a person may experience a gradual sense of loss or change of the energy represented by the planet—again, this may be most dramatic in the case of the outer planets—and it may appear to others that some change in personality has taken place.

Conversely, when a progressed planet stations and turns direct, the person may for the first time experience a facility for expressing overtly the energy associated with the planet. Often, children born with Mercury retrograde, who have experienced being misunderstood, or categorized as "slow," or, in extreme cases, may have manifested some learning disability or autism, catch up to or even surpass their peers when Mercury stations and turns direct by progression. Children born with Mars retrograde may suddenly discover self-confidence or athletic ability for the first time when progressed Mars stations and turns direct. There can often be a sense of liberation, of breaking with the past during this time. Many people, looking back on such a period, will say: "Yes, my life turned right around," or "My thinking changed so much during that year," or "It was about that time I really cut loose." Often, these changes in perspective involve one's faith or personal spiritual journey.

Progressed Aspects

Aspects formed by progressed planets to natal planets or points should be noted. There are few consistent rules for interpretation of progressed aspects, but they very often correspond to times during which there is marked personal growth, often of an emotional nature and requiring adjustment or flexibility of one kind or another. This is especially true if the progressed aspect is supported by a consistent major transit during the months of its activation. The major focus in such cases is on the transit, particularly in the case of a minor progressed aspect. But the progressed aspect corresponds to noteworthy background vibrations.

Any progression to the planetary ruler of the natal chart, or made by the progressed ruling planet to a natal planet or angle, should receive special attention, because of the overall significance of that planet. Again, no rigid rules apply. But keep an eye on this. Turn your conscious gaze towards it. Any aspect, transit or progression which touches the chart ruler can correspond with some very personal issues, fundamental feelings of identity and basic emotional themes. Progressions involving the chart ruler can point to times of subtle or radical change, especially when accompanied by consistent major transits. If so, the period of about six months during which the progression is in effect could mark a key phase, during which issues related to the transit cycles "erupt" or culminate or attract attention in a meaningful way.

Take account also of aspects made between progressed planets or from progressed planets to progressed angles. The same principles apply. Avoid hard-and-fast rules. Consider the nature of the planets and angles involved. Look for significant major transits. Usually, the conjunction is the most significant aspect. Often, however, the various aspects formed by progressed planets during any given year seem to blend together to create a subtle sense of an inner vibration, which may be experienced during that year.

P/Venus Conjunct P/Mars

<%-2>This, and, to a lesser extent, other aspects between these progressed planets, often corresponds to a year or so during which there may be developments in love or other relationships. This is probably due to an increased inner focus on issues of partnership, sex, romance, desire, and so on, which may reflect an inner urge toward experiencing harmony, following through on yearnings, and knowing what one wants in a more powerful way. This progressed conjunction (or the progression of Venus to the natal Sun, Moon, or the progression of the Sun in aspect to natal Venus) seems to occur at times when there are transits which reflect relationship themes.

P/ Moon Conjunct P/Venus or P/Mars

This conjunction can also point to times when there may be developments in love or other relationships. As a lunar progression, the time-scale for this progression is closer to one month than to the six months or one year associated with other progressions. But these progressions, like all lunar progressions, often mark periods of key developmental events or shifts in outlook or feelings, which are catalytic points during larger transit cycles.

P/ Ascendant or MC Conjunct Natal or Progressed Planet

In general, this kind of progression points towards some kind of "awakening," or new light shining on the drive of the planet touched by the progressed Ascendant. Such a conjunction can point to a period of about one year, during which there is a sense of a "new beginning," especially in relation to the drive of the planet being touched by the progressed Ascendant. In the case of a natal planet, the cycle can feel slightly more overt, or have a more conscious quality. On the other hand, the progressed Ascendant conjunct a progressed planet can indicate a more interior, emotional or spiritual process of change. In either case, the cycle can produce significant inner growth, a very personal leg of one's journey, whether spiritual, creative, intuitive, emotional, or all of these.

The conjunction of the progressed MC to a progressed or natal planet can sometimes correspond to times during which there are changes of career, aspirations, identity or role. These progressions, as in all other cases, must be interpreted in the light of the whole picture of what is going on in a chart at any given time. If the progression is to a progressed planet, changes may be more interior—more related to your aspirations or feelings about identity, and adjustments you may be making in terms of your changing role. While this may be also be true in the case of a progression of the MC to a natal planet, these may also correspond to times of definite exterior change in your actual job, self-image or role. Again, no absolute rules apply—your own powers of perception and observation will be your most dynamic interpretive tools.

Additional Thoughts

Whenever you are seeking to interpret any progression, there are some basic questions you can ask:

- What are the other progressions?
- What are the transits?
- What does the natal chart suggest?
- What do you, or your client, feel about the symbols?
- What do you sense or perceive about what is going on in your life and inside youself?

Because, bottom line, these are the most significant kinds of question to be asked during any consideration of transits or progressions. What is ready to be born, to be nurtured, to be healed, to be followed-through-upon, to be let go of, or to be swept away in your life and inside yourself? Interpreting the progressions can stimulate your intuition, and give you a lot of clues and insight into these very personal cycles in your life.

Chapter 15

Transits, Returns and Other Simple Calculations

In this chapter, the last dealing with mathematical calculations, we will consider a few simple, but important techniques for obtaining astrological information. We will explore transits, solar and lunar returns, relocated natal charts, aspects, midpoints, and declinations. The techniques involved in each case are straightforward applications of those we have already discussed, and should occasion no difficulty.

Transits

Transits are the literal positions of the planets, nodes of the Moon, and angles at any given date, time and place, considered relative to the natal chart. They should be written on a wheel outside the natal chart, or outside the natal chart and the progressed chart for the same date and time, so that the aspects from wheel to wheel, and the natal houses through which the planets are transiting, are clear. To calculate transits, construct a natal chart for the given date, time and place. The place will be relocated, usually either to the place where the subject resides, or the place where the reading will be given, though any place may be selected if there is a particular reason to consider it, for example the place of some major event in the subject's life. Use the geographical coordinates of whatever place is selected. The transiting Ascendant and Midheaven should always be calculated, but, as transits are written outside the natal chart, it is unnecessary to calculate other house cusps.

Solar and Lunar Returns

A solar or lunar return chart is a chart erected for the moment at which the Sun or Moon returns to its exact natal position. In the case of the Sun, this is an annual event (popularly known as a birthday) and, in the case of the Moon, a monthly event. The preferred practice is to relocate the chart to the place where the subject was, is or will be residing on the date of the return. So we will use the geographical coordinates for that place.

The only problem is to ascertain the exact time at which the Sun or Moon returned to its natal position. This is done using the familiar method of interpolation using the two closest positions as given in the ephemeris.

As an example, assume that we have been asked to construct a solar return chart for Jane Doe for the year beginning with her "birthday" in 1996, and given that she now resides in Denver, Colorado. (The reason for putting the word birthday in quotes is that a solar return may not fall on the birthday as celebrated by the client in whatever time zone she is now living. It will, however, occur within a day of the birthday. The same is true of lunar returns, even though people do not generally celebrate lunar birthdays.)

For greater accuracy, we will always use the calculated position of the natal Sun, not the rounded-off position we copied on to the wheel. The calculated position of Jane Doe's natal Sun is 29 ♉ 45 39 (the target position). Looking at the ephemeris for May 1996, we see that the Sun returned to this position sometime between midnight

GMT on May 20 and midnight GMT on May 21. The exact time at which this occurred will be the time for which we will construct the return chart. The method is as follows (you can use solar return Worksheet):

1. Note the position of the Sun at midnight GMT on the earlier and later closest dates (May 20 and 21, 1996). Calculate the total travel for this period of 24 hours. Call this T1. As in previous calculations, it will be simpler to express the later position as 30 ♉ rather than 0 ♊.

2. Find the travel between the target position and the closest earlier midnight GMT position, and call this T2.

3. Perform the calculation (T2 / T1) x 24, and add the result to midnight GMT on the earlier date. This will give the GMT time of the solar return.

4. Find the corresponding local standard time and true local time at Denver.

5. Construct a natal chart using the data obtained.

Later position:	30 13 30	Target position:	29 45 39
Earlier position:	29 15 46	Earlier position:	29 15 46
Travel:	57 44		29 53
	(T1)		(T2)

(T2 / T1) x 24 = 12.42263 = 12 hours 25 minutes 21 seconds

GMT time of solar return = May 20, 1996, at 12 25 21 GMT.

Standard time zone for Denver = MST (+7 00 00).

Corresponding standard time at Denver = May 20, 1996, at 05 25 21 MST.

Time zone correction for Denver = 6 59 56 (i.e. it will be minimally later at Denver than at the MST meridian). Therefore, we calculate true local time as follows:

Meridian:	07 00 00
Denver	06 59 56
Local correction:	00 00 04
+ MST	05 25 21
TLT =	05 25 25 on May 20, 1996

We will now construct a natal chart for May 20, 1996, at 05 25 21 MST, at Denver, Colorado. This will be Jane's 1996 solar return chart. All the house cusps must be calculated, as the practice is to use the return as the base chart, and write the natal planets on an outside wheel.

As always, be prepared for a possible change of date with the conversion of GMT to local standard time and true local time. Note also that, on May 20, 1996, MDT was in fact operating in Denver. This does not matter here, because we always work with GMT and local standard time. If we were dealing with an actual birth occurring in Denver at this time, a clock would record the birth time in MDT, and we would have to subtract an hour to convert to MST. In working with our return chart, this was unnecessary, because our data were obtained in standard time.

The same procedure can be followed for a lunar return chart (or, for that matter, a chart for the return of any planet) substituting the position of the Moon or the planet concerned.

Relocated Natal Charts

A relocated natal chart is employed to assess the effect which might be produced if the subject relocates to a given place. The procedure is to construct a natal chart for the place in question, but using the subject's exact birth data, including the time of birth at the birth place. The object is to produce an essentially hypothetical chart for the same moment in time, but a different place. Thus, if we wish to advise Jane Doe about the possible effects of changing her residence to Auckland, New Zealand, we would construct a natal chart for May 21, 1945, at 11:42

p.m. CWT, using the geographical coordinates of Auckland. We would then convert her local ST birth time to the local ST at Auckland, and calculate the true local time at Auckland in the usual way. This is the only tricky point. Do not use a time of 11:42 p.m. Auckland time! We want the actual moment of birth, regardless of the change in location. Use 11:42 p.m. CWT, and convert this to Auckland time. The result of the relocation will be to alter the Ascendant, the Midheaven and the other house cusps, though, because the time is exactly the same, the planetary positions by sign and degree will be unaffected. The effect of a relocated chart is simply to alter the angles, and so reposition the planets in different houses. Because this is likely to affect their house placement as between angular, succedent and cadent houses, the effect may be considerable. But their sign positions will be unaltered.

Aspects and Midpoints

With a certain amount of practice, major aspects become fairly easy to find by scanning a chart. But with minor aspects, or if you like to be strict in applying certain orbs, the scanning method is less easy. You may prefer to use the method shown below for calculating the exact distance between the planets and points in the chart. The method consists of finding the distance of each planet or point from a fixed point of 0 degrees of Aries. You may recall that we learned this system as one method of finding the position of the Part of Fortune and progressed Midheaven. Any fixed point (for example, the degree of the Sun's position in the chart) could also be used, but the 0 Aries system is far easier, because 0 degrees of each successive sign has a value of 30 more than the preceding sign. For example, 0 degrees of Taurus has a value of 30, 0 degrees of Gemini a value of 60, and so on around the wheel to 0 Pisces, which has a value of 330 degrees. Let us express the position of Jane's natal Sun using this system. The Sun is at 29 ♉ 45 39. We know that 0 Taurus = 30 degrees from the fixed point of 0 Aries, so all we have to do is add 29 45 39, which gives us a value for the Sun of 59 45 39.

For all practical purposes involving aspects, it will be precise enough to use the rounded-off values of the planets, and this is done in the illustration below. If you wish to use the precise calculated positions, remember that the positions of the luminaries are expressed in degrees, minutes and seconds, whereas those of the planets are expressed in degrees and decimalized minutes. Decide which you prefer to work in, and convert the other values accordingly.

☉ 29 ♉ 45 =	59 45	♅ 12 ♊ 24 =	72 24
☽ 25 ♍ 01	175 01	♆ 3 ♎ 49 =	183 49
☿ 5 ♉ 59 =	35 59	♀ 7 ♌ 08 =	127 08
♀ 20 ♈ 47 =	20 47	♄ 27 ♍ 09 =	177 09
♂ 14 ♈ 01 =	14 01	MC 3 ♏ 28 =	213 28
♃ 17 ♍ 35 =	167 35	Asc 15 ♑ 54 =	285 54
♄ 8 ♋ 36 =	98 36	☊ 10 ♋ 01 =	100 01
		☋ 10 ♑ 01 =	280 01

To find the distance between any two planets or points is a matter of subtraction. The answer will be precise enough to tell you whether the distance is within your preferred orb for a particular aspect. For example, to find the distance and aspect between the Sun and Moon, we would simply deduct the lesser value from the greater: (175 01 - 59 45) = 115 16, which is well within orb for a trine.

Bear in mind, however, that the greatest distance involved in any aspect is the opposition, i.e. 180 degrees. Other aspects are based on the shorter arc between two planets or points, the sextile being 60 degrees, the square 90 degrees, and so on. When we measure each planet from a fixed point, such as 0 Aries, the distance between two planets may obviously be expressed as more than 180 degrees, producing an answer of more than 180 degrees when you subtract. This means that you have calculated the longer arc between the two planets or points, instead of the shorter arc on which the aspect is based.

The simplest way to correct this is to deduct the answer from 360 (the total number of degrees in the wheel). This will give you the shorter arc, i.e. distance and aspect. For example, to find the distance between Mars and the Ascendant, we would first subtract as usual. (285 54 - 14 01) = 271 53. Because the answer exceeds 180, this is the longer arc. The shorter arc is (360 00 - 271 53) = 88 07. This is well within orb for a square, which is easily confirmed by scanning the chart - obviously, Mars is square to the Ascendant to an orb of less than 2 degrees. It is unnecessary to make this correction when, although the answer exceeds 180 degrees, it is within your preferred orb for an opposition, e.g. 185 degrees. In all other cases, the shorter arc must be found.

The same system will yield midpoints equally well. To find the midpoint between any two planets, calculate the shorter arc using the methods given above, divide the shorter arc by 2, and add the result to the lower number. As an example, let us find the midpoint of Saturn and Jupiter:

Jupiter =	167 35
Saturn =	98 36
Distance =	68 59

/2 =	34 29 (ignoring seconds)
+ Saturn	98 36
Midpoint =	133 05 = 13 ♌ 05

Declinations

For most purposes, we concentrate on the positions of the planets in the signs. The distance between planets in terms of degrees of signs is longitudinal, i.e. the distance is observed in the sky as running generally east-west. However, it is also possible to measure a distance between planets in terms of how far north (N) or south (S) the planets are of the celestial equator—a latitudinal distance. The latitudinal position of a planet at any given time is known as its declination, and is expressed in degrees and minutes (N) or (S). By no means all astrologers make use of declinations, and, accordingly, not all ephemerises give them. The Rosicrucian ephemeris provides them on a daily basis. There are also tables of correspondences between longitudinal (sign) position and declinations. Any planets which are within (traditionally) one degree of orb in the same hemisphere (i.e. both N or both S) are described as parallel, an aspect which bears some resemblance to a conjunction. Any planets which are within one degree of orb in different hemispheres (i.e. one N and one S) are described as contraparallel, an aspect which bears some resemblance to an opposition. The normal range of declination is between 0 and 23 30 degrees N or S (23 30 degrees being the angle of tilt of the earth's axis).

As in the case of sign position, the outer planets have only a small daily variation in declination, so that, for all normal purposes, the declination at midnight GMT or other time specified in the ephemeris may be used. However, because of the small orb allowed for the parallel and contra-parallel aspects, the precise declination of the luminaries and inner planets should always be caclulated. This is done using the familiar method of interpolation, exactly as in the case of planetary sign position. As an example, let us find the declination of Jane Doe's natal Moon. The method is as follows:

1. Find the Moon's declination at Midnight GMT on the Greenwich birth date (May 21, 1945) and the following day;

2. Find the difference between the two (travel over the 24-hour period);

3. Divide the travel by 24 and multiply by the decimalized GMT birth time (4.7);

4. If the declination is increasing (i.e. the later declination is greater than the earlier) add the result to the earlier declination; if the declination is decreasing (i.e. the earlier is greater) subtract the result from the earlier declination.

Declination midnight May 21:	7 N 26
Declination midnight May 22:	2 N 53
Travel:	4 33
(Travel / 24) x 4.7 = 0 54 (rounded up)	

Earlier declination:	7 N 26 (decreasing)
- travel	0 54
Declination of Moon:	6 N 32

Worksheets
for
Natal Charts
Progressed Charts
Solar Returns

NATAL CHART WORKSHEET 1
Birth Data

Name: Source of data:

Date of birth:

Time of birth (incl. time zone):

Place of birth:

Latitude: Longitude: Time zone correction:
                                                          (long x 4 mins.)

TLT calculation

Clock birth time:

- 1 hour if DT/WT:

_____

Local standard birth time:

+/- mins. of time zone corr::

_____

TLT=

GMT birth time calculation

Method 1	*Method 2*
TLT:	Local standard time:
Time zone corr:	Interval from GMT:
(+ if W of Greenwich - if E of Greenwich)	

GMT birth time =

_____   _____

NATAL CHART WORKSHEET 2
Sidereal time calculation

Sid. time at Greenwich
midnight previous to TLT:

+/- longitude corr: long corr in secs = 2/3 long of place of birth
_____   + W of Greenwich, - if E

Corrected sid. time:

+ interval
TLT-previous midnight:

+ acceleration of interval::   = 10 secs/hour, 1 sec/6 mins of interval
_____

Calculated sid. time:

Note: add 12 hours for Southern Hemisphere birth

Closest sid. times in table of houses: earlier: later:

Sidereal time factor calculation

Calculated sid. time:

- closest earlier sid. time:
_____

Difference in seconds:

STF = (difference/240) =

Latitude factor calculation

Minutes of latitude:

LF = (minutes of latitude/60) =

NATAL CHART WORKSHEET 3

House cusps: Sidereal time adjustment

Closest sid times: earlier: later:

Closest latitudes: lower: higher:

STF =

Use lower latitude:

	10(MC)	11	12	1(Asc)	2

3

cusp later
sid. time:

cusp earlier
sid. time:

_____

Distance in
minutes:

Distance
x STF

_____

Sid. time
correction:

+ mins. of cusp
earlier sid. time:

_____

Cusp adjusted
for sid. time:

Final 10th house cusp =

NATAL CHART WORKSHEET 4

House cusps: Latitude adjustment

Closest sid. times: earlier: later:

Closest latitudes: lower: higher:

LF =

Use earlier sid. time:

	11	12	1(Asc)	2	3
cusp at higher lat:					
cusp at lower lat:					
Distance in mins:					
Distance *x* LF					
LF correction:					

Cusp adjusted
for sid. time:
(from p.3)
+/- latitude
correction:
(If higher is
higher, add)

Corrected cusps:

Final cusps (rounded up or down):

Note: reverse for Southern Hemisphere birth

10	11	12	1	2	3
4	5	6	7	8	9

NATAL CHART WORKSHEET 5

Planetary positions: Luminaries

GMT birth time: Decimalized:
GMT birth date:

                       ☉   ☽

Position midnight
day after GMT birth date:

Position midnight
GMT birth date:

_____

Distance in 24 hours:

(Distance/24) *x*
interval birth time -
previous midnight:

_____

Actual travel:

Starting position
(midnight birth date):

+ actual travel:

_____

Position:

NATAL CHART WORKSHEET 6

Planetary positions: Inner planets

GMT birth time: Decimalized:
GMT birth date:

	☿	♀	♂
Position midnight day after GMT birth date:			
Position midnight GMT birth date:			
Distance in 24 hours:			
(Distance/24) *x* interval birth time - previous midnight:			
Actual travel:			
Starting position (midnight birth date):			
+ actual travel (- *if retrograde)*			
Position:			

NATAL CHART WORKSHEET 7

Planetary positions: ♃ ♄ ♅

GMT birth time: Decimalized:

GMT birth date:

             ♃   ♄   ♅

Position midnight
day after GMT birth date:

Position midnight
GMT birth date:

Distance in 24 hours:

(Distance/24) *x*
interval birth time -
previous midnight:

Actual travel:

Starting position
(midnight birth date):

+ actual travel
(- if retrograde)

Position:

NATAL CHART WORKSHEET 8

Plantary positions: Ψ ♀ ☊

GMT birth time: Decimalized:
GMT birth date:

	Ψ	♀	☊
Position midnight day after GMT birth date:			
Position midnight GMT birth date:			
Distance in 24 hours:			
(Distance/24) *x* interval birth time - previous midnight:			
Actual travel:			
Starting position (midnight birth date):			
+ actual travel: *(- if retrograde)*			
Position:			

Position of ☋ =

NATAL CHART WORKSHEET 9
Chiron, Part of Fortune, Part of Spirit

ⵣ

Position 1st day of month after birth month::

Position 1st day birth month:

_____

Distance in month:

(Distance/number of days in month) *x*
number of birth date:

_____

Actual travel:

Starting position (1st day of birth month):

+ actual travel:
(- if retrograde)

_____

Position:

⊗   ♍

(Diurnal charts - reverse for nocturnal)

Ascendant: Ascendant:

+ Moon   + Sun

_____   _____

- Sun   - Moon

_____   _____

Position:

PROGRESSIONS WORKSHEET 1

Name:

Date and Time of Birth (at Greenwich):

Midnight Date Calculation

Sidereal time at midnight Greenwich
for *Greenwich* birth date:

- Birth time (GMT):

_____

+ acceleration of birth time:
(10 secs/hour, 1 sec/6 mins.):

_____

Sidereal time for birth (STB) =

Midnight date = closest earlier ST =   Same / previous year?

Time:

    ST later day: STB:

    - ST earlier day: - ST earlier day:

    _____   _____
            (ST1)   (ST2)

Time = [(ST2 / ST1) x 24] + midnight, earlier date =

PROGRESSIONS WORKSHEET 2

Correlation of years with dates
(Greenwich birth date = year in which midnight date falls, then 1 day = 1 year)

Date = *Year*   *Date* = *Year*   *Date* = *Year*

Calculation of progressed MC

Progressed Sun:

- Natal Sun:
_____

Solar arc =

+ Natal MC
_____

Prog MC =

PROGRESSIONS WORKSHEET 3
Progressed planetary positions for target date/time

Target date = Day #   Midnight date = Day #
Time   (GMT)   Time   (GMT)

Difference (n) = _____   (Decimalized =   )

                                       ☉   ☽

Position on later year day:

Position on earlier year day:

Travel: _____

[(Travel/365) x n] =

+ position on earlier day:

Position on target date=   _____

                        ☿   ♀   ♂

Position on later year day:

Position on earlier year day:
(Reverse if ℞)

Travel: _____

[(Travel/365) x n} =

+ position on earlier day:
(- if ℞)   _____
Position on target date =

PROGRESSIONS WORKSHEET 4

To find date/time progressed planet reaches target position

Midnight date = Day #   Time:

Target between midnight date _____ (earlier year) and _____ (later year)

Position on later day: Target Position:

-Position on earlier day: -Position on earlier day:

Travel (T1):   Travel (T2):

(If ʀ, T1 = earlier-later, T2 = earlier-target)

[(T2 / T1) x 365) =   (Days/time)

+ midnight date/time:

Target date/time =

To find date of progressed lunation

Date of lunation: Day #   Degree of lunation:
Time of lunation   (GMT)
Midnight date = Day #   Time:

Target between midnight date _____(earlier year) and _____ (later year)

(Time of lunation / 24) x 365 =   (Days/time)

+ midnight date/time:

Date/time of prog. lunation =

PROGRESSIONS WORKSHEET 5
Calculation of progressed Asc

Progressed MC =   *Southern hemisphere, reverse =*

Closest MCs in table houses to prog MC = earlier: later:

Distance earlier - later =   mins. (D1)

Distance earlier- prog MC =   mins. (D2)

Using lower latitude:

Asc for later sidereal time:

Asc for earlier sidereal time:

Distance in mins. (D3) =   _____

$(D2 / D1) \times D3 =$ (D4)

Asc for earlier sidereal time:

+ D4

Unadjusted Asc =   _____

Using earlier sidereal time:

Asc at higher lat:

Asc at lower lat:

Distance in mins =   _____

x latitude factor

(mins of lat/60) =   (latitude correction)

Unadjusted Asc:

+/- Lat corr:

 (if higher is higher, add)

_____

 Prog Asc =   *(Southern hemisphere, reverse)*

SOLAR RETURN WORKSHEET 1
To find date and time of return

Natal Sun position =

Position midnight later: Natal position:

Position midnight earlier   Position midnight earlier:

Travel: (T1)   (T2)

Date and time of return = [(T2 / T1) x 24] + earlier midnight:

Date =

Time =   (GMT)

Place of residence at time of return:

Latitude: Longitude:

(Calculate natal chart for above values)

About the Authors

Peter Murphy, M.A., LL.B., PMAFA is a native of England. He practices and teaches astrology with his wife Chris in Texas. A number of his articles have been published in *The Mountain Astrologer* and *Today's Astrologer*. Peter is a law graduate of the University of Cambridge, England, and is a professor of law at South Texas College of Law. He specializes in the inter-relationship of law and astrology and the resolution of legal issues through astrology.

Beth Rosato, D.F. Astrol. S., MAFA has maintained a diverse astrological counseling practice for many years. An international columnist, freelance writer and author of three other books (*Astrology of Dreams*, *Equal Houses* and co-author of *First Survive, Then Thrive*), Beth is a New York resident, and has served as the head tutor in North America for the Faculty of Astrological Studies, London, England.